Pearls in the Web ar[illegible]tions

All characters are fictional. Any similarity to any actual person is purely coincidental.

ISBN: 978-178456-758-3
Paperback

First published 2021 by Upfront Publishing
Peterborough, England.

An environmentally friendly book printed and bound in England
by www.printondemand-worldwide.com

Pearls in the Web and Other Reflections:

Thoughts on
Nature and
Spirituality

Peter Quince

Arboretum Press

CONTENTS

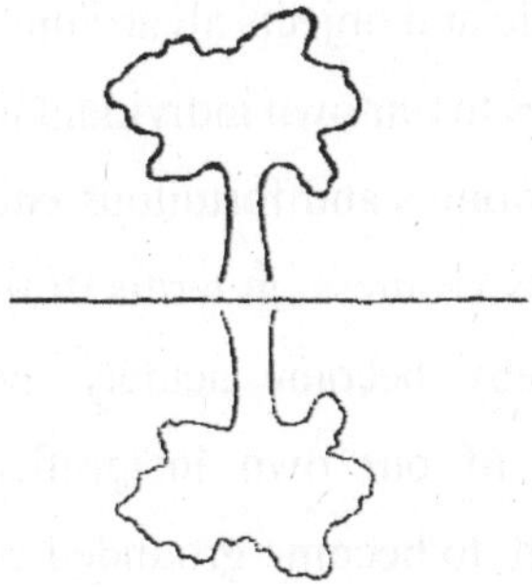

1 INTRODUCTION

Stand and listen to the universe, I was once told.
So I did. What I perceived was not the music of the spheres... but silence.

I have for many years cultivated an interest in the Taoist belief in the interconnectedness of everything in the cosmos, from the tiniest particle to unimaginably massive planets; from viruses to great whales. I began to understand that energy rather than matter lies at the heart of what is; that a mechanistic view of reality is inadequate; and that mind is all. But such concepts are huge, indeed overwhelming.

How can we, on a personal level, appreciate this undoubted interconnectedness? How can we become one with the animate and inanimate, the life and objects all around us? One answer is to relate holistic realities to our own individual lives, our perceptions, our rituals and ceremonies and fortuitous encounters; to perceive the cosmos, for all its vastness, in terms of the personal, even the mundane, and thereby become acutely aware, in marvellous moments of satori, of our own insignificant but nonetheless thrilling part. In short, to become grounded even as we fly.

I am an enthusiastic gardener who has the good fortune to cultivate a substantial plot. In one sense I regard my garden as the world in miniature: all life is there. Whilst immersing myself in the practical pursuit of cultivation, I have become aware, in epiphanic moments, of the magic of plants, animals and the very fabric of the earth itself.

I have highlighted a whole series of incidents, moments and reflections, which others leading busy lives may pass by, and tried to discover a deeper meaning in these encounters. I have sought to capture them in little cameos, gained invaluable insights, and turned experience into print. I am still not entirely sure if that is a wise thing to do; but writing, of course, clarifies thought and is a way of making sense.

I have become aware whilst performing tai chi on the lawn of a vixen's proximate curiosity; cradled a quiescent collared dove until it flew lustily from my hands; rescued a blue tit from panicked self-captivity in a shed; raised a dead but flawless Red

Admiral from sepulchral grass (and venerate, six years on, its perfectly preserved remains); contemplated in wonder the tiniest of snails, dormant in the half curl of a wintry jasmine bush; and marvelled at the pearls of moisture picked out by early sunlight embroidering the shimmer of a spider's web.

I celebrate the spirits of trees, which I feel an impulse to commune with and draw; become an innocent 'lunatic' in the face of the full moon; watch Tibetan monks create with unbelievable patience a sand mandala; astonish myself at the majestic sight of black swans on a monastery pond; listen to the echoes of ancestral voices in a Zen garden; and touch on the environmental, transcendent, sometimes earthy, sometimes mystical beliefs of Thoreau and Edward Abbey.

These and many other experiences have convinced me that, far from being separate and isolated individuals, as perhaps many of us feel on a daily basis, we are one with the universe, indivisible and unbroken. We just need to tune in, stand back, give ourselves time and presence. What appears fragmented is really a continuum, a great matrix of energy, filling space and time and generating love.

In these essays I seek to convey, through chance encounters with vixen and snail, forsythia bonsai and tame robin, the delightful realisation that all is part of one great flux; and the silence which surrounds us is a stupendous and beautiful mystery.

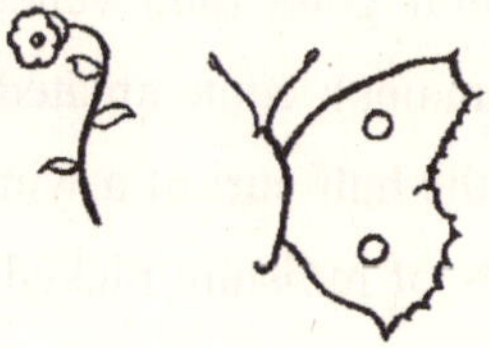

2 MAGICAL BUTTERFLY

A fallen flower
returning to the branch?
It was a butterfly.

It must have been five summers ago. I was strolling on my lawn when something very bright, multi-coloured and luminescent shone from the uniform green of the grass: a Red Admiral, sitting, resting with wings outstretched - or so I thought. I was charmed. I stopped in my tracks, crouched before this liminal jewel, expecting it to flutter away. But it didn't; it didn't move.

This beautiful creature, I soon discovered, was dead. It sent a little frisson of shock through me. But I became entranced nonetheless. Such perfection, such absolute stillness, such final unfathomable poise. My initial joy was tinged with sorrow. I wished that, full of life, it had alighted from the lawn and danced in the air and delighted me with its delicate, coquettish antics, as many had done that summer.

I love butterflies for their otherworldly nature, their mercurial characteristics, their ephemeral fragility which, I suspect, conceals a transcendent strength; their innocent mimickry of lighter-than-air spirits, not the spirits of the dead but very much the spirits of the living.

In those few moments of contemplation, a brief episode when my lawn became a kind of shrine, I felt, oddly, that my spirit had transferred into the Red Admiral. I wished to revivify it, to will it into fresh life, to witness its resurrection.

Of course the mundane, being what it is, my hopes were soon dashed. That perfect creature, with its orange bars and white flecks, remained inert, as if in contemplation of eternity. But – and this is crucial – there did exist a connection between us, something beyond words, some force infusing the living and the dead.

As tenderly as I could I lifted the butterfly and held it in my open palm and brought it close to my face. I was mesmerised, both saddened and joyful, wondering what I should do with such a divine arrangement of contours and colours. The Red Admiral appeared undamaged; I wondered why it had died, and then recalled the awful brevity of a butterfly's lifespan. So often along with beauty goes ephemerality: all things must pass. It made me think of my own mortality; how one day I too, broken and exhausted, would be able to dance no more.

I took the Red Admiral into my house, palm open, staring down at it reverently. It felt to me like an improvised and very private funeral, an acknowledgement of something wondrous that I had happened upon. But I could not bear to bury this almost insubstantial corpse. It retained every jot of its living beauty, which I could not bear to hide or crumple. So I preserved it and painted it in watercolours; that was my impulse, my tribute to what many would no doubt call an insignificant creature, a moment's passing, an instantly replicable member of its kind.

I stood the watercolour, a paltry reproduction, a pale shadow of the real thing, on my bureau; and I placed the Red Admiral itself on a small piece of white card just in front of the watercolour. It seemed surreal; the painting and the butterfly in close proximity. But, due to my poor art, not quite mirror images.

That was five summers ago. The creature sits there yet, undiminished, undamaged, unembalmed but clearly as resplendent as the day it died.

Whenever I enter the study I glance at the Red Admiral and take a brief look at my inadequate reproduction of it, a result, perhaps, more of love than judgement. And then I feel that, magically, unfathomably, beyond all sense of reason – because much of the mystery of life is beyond all reason – that exquisite little creature, years beyond its capricious fluttering in the physical world, the embodied world, flutters in my soul and provides me with a gift of insight, a moment of remembered satori, an entry into another world where life and death are commingled in a complex but entrancing dance of their own.

And I feel, in the face of a butterfly's exquisite being, humbled.

3 PEARLS IN THE WEB

First gleam of sunrise;
the shock of recognition;
infinite wisdom.

The plum tree stood in a big tub at the end of the garden. Overnight there had been little rain, but dawn broke bright and sunny. I went to check on a few bonsai trees, how they had taken the beneficence of rain in their ultramarine dishes. But what took my eye was something else, something quite unexpected.

The 'Plum Glory' tree, for that was the variety, had borne sweet, tiny fruits earlier in the summer, but now virtually all its leaves had fallen like golden scimitars on the tub's dark compost. I was prepared to ignore it, bypass it; it was done with. But I couldn't. The sight that greeted me was so arresting.

Why had I chosen to ignore this tree on so many previous occasions, simply because it had served its practical purpose in providing us with three months' worth of plums? It had yielded its silent offerings, given up its bounty, remained true to its nature, asked nothing in return except water and a modicum of feed and a little light pruning the previous winter. And, thoughtlessly, in a slew of early morning sun, I had almost breezed past it to the low wall where bonsai stood in a neat, serrated line.

Sunshine, particularly when low-angled at dawn, or in anticipation of dusk, can produce the most surreal effects; it can stop one in one's tracks with stunning optical illusions. On that otherwise unremarkable morning something remarkable happened whilst most of the human world was barely stirring from nocturnal slumbers. (Are dreams less real than the waking world?)

I recognised something which, though it lives always in my soul, often lies buried too deep for conscious awareness. That is, the interconnectedness of all things, the matrix beyond mere mathematics. The potted plum tree, shorn of fruit and leaves and bare-branched, was in its mute fashion telling me something manifested in its spectacular adornments.

A spider had been at work. A spider linking tree with human with sunlight with… how many other things? Instantly, faced with this transformative vision, I forgot the original purpose of my visit to the end of the garden.

The plum tree had been decked out with at least half a dozen exquisite spiders' webs. An incredibly industrious spider had been busy weaving a series of lacy shawls all across the plum tree. In prodigious sunlight each eye-level web, perfect in itself, was hung with pearls of dew, glistening and shimmering in the slightest of breezes.

I was mesmerised, taken aback, seized with wonder. How many millions of times must such webs have been created overnight by how many millions of spiders? Such a seemingly mundane process, such a private enterprise, seemed to have been produced just for me on that one otherwise ordinary morning of the year. And yet, of course, this skein of webs was not woven around the plum tree for me. Far from it. Nothing in the garden is achieved for the purpose of pleasing me or anyone else; the object is not to please but to live. But, fortuitously, I reaped the benefit whilst most of the human world was slumbering.

What did it mean for me, this chance happening? It gave me joy, induced in me a profound awareness, reiterated the beauty of the natural world in all its minute and easily overlooked ramifications. The usual veil of ignorance was lifted, just for a few cathartic moments.

I stood gazing from a distance of three feet or so at the Plum

Glory, which serendipitously contained within its weave of branches a new coat of glory all its own, not of many colours but of phosphorescent silver.

Each drop of dew which clung to the threads shone like a liquid pearl and trembled, as if it had absorbed the sun's first burst of energy and transformed it into a light show. That spider, like some spontaneous window-dresser, had completed its work, its wheels of light, to perfection, and had now retreated to a fork or fissure within the complex of branches, primed to pounce, ready for a well-deserved meal. That was my assumption, and that is raw life in miniature.

The display was left for me to marvel at – and I did. I wanted to witness, to luxuriate, in this free show of stunning beauty; but I knew that many other people, even if awake that early and venturing to some corner of the garden, would perhaps sleepily and fleetingly glance at those pearls of light and dismiss them as nothing more than.... well, spiders' webs!

But I was enchanted, struck anew with a sudden realisation: the interconnectedness of all things sentient and insentient; the way that so much life goes on under the radar, so to speak; how much we humans miss, or dismiss; how our ignorance is greater than our knowledge; how much beauty passes us by because we are insufficiently awake or too distracted to notice.

I know that that spider, temporary resident of my plum tree, had constructed those webs – a whole intricate series of them – because it could do no other in order to provide food for itself. That is its instinct, its destiny, its ceaseless toil. And I suspect, furthermore, that it hadn't the slightest notion of the visual beauty it had created, let alone that some human being who 'owned' the plum tree would stop and stare and admire both the spider's acrobatic ingenuity and its unconscious art.

But I am grateful that, for a few moments a confluence of sunlight, expertly woven threads, morning dew and someone just awake enough to pay close attention, enabled an obscure little fragment of life to emblazon itself in the memory.

I knew that later the same day, when conditions changed, those webs would somehow lose their dawning magic. It needed a single moment – that moment and no other – to afford me a privileged vision of pearls in the web.

4 THOREAU RECONSIDERED

Many lands, one race
share this bonding latitude,
this round longitude.

I have a universe in my garden. So Thoreau might have said. It is not such a fanciful idea. Another nineteenth-century American, Walt Whitman, declared that he 'contained multitudes'. Quite so. I do not pretend to attain to anything like the stature of those two men, but I do sense the cosmological significance of my one small, verdant plot. My garden contains multitudes and, like Whitman, is full of fascinating contradictions. As I am. As we probably all are.

But it is Thoreau, above all others, who illuminates the vitality of the soil, the need to belong to a place – one favoured place –

and the compulsion to celebrate simplicity.

When people say to me, 'Why don't you go abroad on holiday? Why don't you explore the big wide world, find new things, indulge in novel pleasures?' and so on, I have a ready-made reply which might sound glib, even precious. But it is sincere if a little eccentric.

'I can explain the big wide world in my own garden; it is always changing; it contains mountain ranges, forests, plains, tundra, glaciers, lakes, rivers and semi desert.' At different times of year, of course, and on a vastly reduced physical scale.

'I find new things every time I venture to some corner of the garden I have not visited for some time. The pleasure afforded me from doing this is considerable and, in imagination, lasting.'

My garden contains frontiers which are porous and allow unrestricted immigration. Foxes, hedgehogs, snails, mice, squirrels and busy armies of ants roam the varying terrain. Bees, wasps, dragonflies, butterflies, all manner of birds and meteoric bats overfly my territory, which is 'mine' only in the legal, strictly human sense. I have no exclusion zone. I understand that these non-human citizens, in one form or another, were here long before I was, and will remain here when I go.

The unwritten constitution of my property allows for all kinds of settlements, some temporary, some more or less permanent –

that is, if I don't dig, scarify, fell, prune and rake too much.

I am happy to arrange for verdant accommodation, within limits, of course, as I do need land for my own fruit, flowers and vegetables, some of which is shared with hungry, opportunist creatures. I once heard an intriguing suggestion: the construction of a 'bee hotel', with certain similarities to a bird house, which would welcome solitary bees at a peppercorn rent. My garden supports a symbiotic population of nomads, cave-dwellers and monastics.

To return to Thoreau.

He employed the mantra 'Simplify! Simplify! Simplify!' (yes, three times), and wondered why friends encouraged him to travel in order to 'broaden the mind'. 'But my mind is already as broad as I can make it,' he might have said, as I would say today. Thoreau contended that on his limited acreage, borrowed from his friend and fellow Transcendentalist Emerson, he would 'live deliberately', by which I take him to mean mindfully, with as great an awareness of surrounding nature as possible. And, furthermore, he desired to be fully awake and live life to the limit – because this is the only one we have and sooner or later each of us will descend into darkness. It is the Stoic philosophy with the addition of garden produce.

Thoreau was in fact testing himself. He was exploring how he could live well: sheltered, clothed, fed and watered, lauding the basic necessities. And, although in his day he would not have expressed it in such words, with as light an ecological footprint as possible. I'm sure that when he died he would not have wished anything of himself left behind except a log cabin, a foolproof philosophy and the wind.

If Thoreau – a colossal inspiration for ecologists, environmentalists and simple-lifers in time to come – were to be miraculously resurrected (fanciful notion!) and survey with his hawk-like eye the earth today, what he would find would make his heart bleed. What he would all too soon discover would be the earth – our only home – close to its death throes in consequence of some obscene terminal illness. And what he would conclude, as I do, is that our troublesome and short-sighted species has perpetrated an unforgivable crime upon our kind and all the abundance of life-forms on the planet.

My garden is my universe, as Thoreau's few acres were his. I do not wish to build on it, concrete it over, create a billiard-table lawn, sluice it with toxins or make a profit from it, except such profit as may feed my family and enable us to put a little by. What delights in the summer sustains through the winter.

Thoreau knew that the real secret of living was to cultivate an intimate connection with the natural world and pay respectful attention to everything within it. That way no mindless desecration can be perpetrated and we should live within our means and our consciences.

Although his log cabin no longer stands beside Walden Pond, his spirit most certainly does. And although I may not have seen much of the world, I have travelled the universe of my back garden countless times and celebrated the vibrant community I find there.

I hope that, like Thoreau, I have been sufficiently awake.

5 SACRED SILENCE

Stillness, silence, night.
Death and life in either scale,
Hang, wait, equipoised.

The modern world is full of chatter. This cannot be a healthy thing, because in the midst of the babble of voices, the relentless bombardment of information, what we risk losing are our essential selves. What we forfeit is the stillness, silence and sacred essence at the very centre of each of us. Indigenous peoples, in particular, celebrated these virtues, and perhaps those few we have left untouched still do.

These are fragile realities which must inevitably be disturbed by the cataclysm of noise that greets us every day and constantly serves to draw us away from the divine within us. Spirits do not appreciate disturbance. Within the realms of silence you discover that, paradoxically, you are privileged to hear what was drowned out before. You come fully to yourself, as it were, and experience a sensation of regaining the soul, something that is always utterly moving and cathartic.

The technological maelstrom that we find ourselves in the midst of encourages a culture of speed, acquisition, consumption and shrill discourse – all enemies of the slowness, simplicity and silence that were the hallmarks of our ancestors' lives. We have largely lost those things, subsumed as we are in a cauldron of other people's soundtracks and intrusive conversations – unless we take active and mindful steps to restore the balance and gain the wholesomeness bestowed by a regime of quietude; or at least those murmurous, therapeutic sounds which accentuate silence.

It is possible to restore that balance – but only if we step aside from the frantic and superficial demands of the modern world, at least for significant periods of time, and rediscover our quintessential being. There are ways of achieving this, and I know of retreats with exquisite gardens* which are perfect examples of locations where inner peace, stillness and silence may be experienced to such a degree that one begins to feel miraculously restored, and in addition sense a connection with the cosmos, the universal soul whose vast and profound silence is symbolised most enchantingly, for example, by a full moon on a still night. I wonder how many people in the modern world, relentlessly distracted, are more than minimally aware of the magic of the full moon, or the blessings of starry darkness in an ocean of man-made nocturnal glare.

We stuff music into our ears at our peril; we are mesmerised by seductive and rapidly changing images at huge spiritual cost; we pay heed to the formless, superficial blandishments of advertising to our detriment. Everyone wants our attention; everyone wants to tell us something; everyone wants a piece of us, or attempts to sell us what we don't need.

Beyond all this psychic perturbation lies silence, like a blessed balm, a soothing lotion, a portal into the profundity of the self; not so much an escape from the world as an entry into its real significance, its numinous nature. Down there where the waters spring forth and trickle with unobtrusive music and begin to soothe our troubled hearing. As Buddha said: 'Do not speak – unless it improves on silence.'

You can keep the chatter at bay, at least for a time, by listening only to the beat of your heart, the rhythms of the natural world and the ministrations of your soul. I would like, finally, to offer you a sacred, silent blessing – beyond words, of course.

* Chalice Well in Glastonbury is a stunning example of a retreat with an exquisite, aesthetic, spiritually nourishing and utterly tranquil garden, which contains a sacred well and healing waters. I would recommend an extended visit to those who value silence and deep connection with the earth.

6 CHANCE ENCOUNTER

This creature spies me,
shares early sun, mesmerised
between breath and breath.

This summer has seen so many warm, sunny days and pure blue skies, and my garden seems to have collared most of them. I do not wish to be selfish – I am willing to share the sun with anyone – but I kind of regard that first hour of the day, when the slant rays of the ascending sun kiss my garden and reflect its surfaces like a many-faceted diamond, as my own. Is that selfish? Not really. The sun blesses us all and what's more links us intimately wherever we happen to be in the world.

Let me tell you about one particular morning, very early, just after first light. I am in the habit of doing tai chi first thing and feel obliged to do so indoors in winter, when the weather's wet or chilly. This summer, drawn by unusual warmth and crystalline light in the dawn-breaking garden, I often ventured down to an expanse of lawn between my greenhouse and a high hedge, a place of particular resonance.

One cloudless and utterly still morning, before six o'clock, I stood facing east with closed eyes. Already the bright sun gave an aura to the wigwam of beans and reflected off the greenhouse glass and sensuously warmed my face.

I stood in silent meditation. The only sounds were birdsong and the murmur of the sea in my ears. It felt vital and mysterious and, for a fleeting moment, I wished others to come and experience the joy that I felt, a sense of the numinous, a profound connectivity.

But I was equally happy with a sort of solitude which, paradoxically, convinced me that I was far from alone. I was in the midst of multitudes. I was removed from human company but not from Nature. It is a great wonder to stand in the maelstrom of life, comprise a miniscule fragment, and sense at once the turning of the Earth.

Standing barefoot on the lawn, slowly opening my eyes, catching sight of the sun's peeping and unobstructed rays, I felt what I can only describe as an intense groundedness, a belonging and a heightened sensitivity. My awareness seemed to soar.

When I had completed the tai chi form I moved very slowly, with great deliberation, around familiar nooks of the garden, aware of far more than, as a muck-and-mulch gardener, I am normally aware of.

I studied spiders' webs which reflected sunlight through clinging moisture; I observed with unusual clarity the fascinating features of a snail and the rhythms of its miniscule antennae; I gazed long at resting butterflies, their wings semi-transparent, like finest gossamer; and little shimmering spirals of gnats rising and falling.

In the near silence all seemed surpassingly beautiful, at once chaotic and yet ordered. It felt like a homecoming. Finally I stood still beneath the benediction of the sun, closed my eyes once more, insatiable, drinking in the world through my senses.

When at long last I opened my eyes, something appeared in my peripheral vision. I turned my head with practised slowness. A fox stood staring up at me; she was no more than six feet away. We shared a moment's silence, a rare connection, eye contact. When she walked away, unhurried, behind a shed, I felt the hairs prickle on my neck. I felt both privileged and transformed.

The image of that vixen and what the chance meeting meant remains with me to this day.

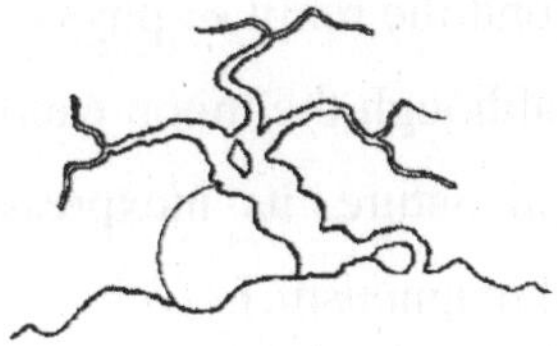

7 MOONSONG

The moon's slender arms
offer the sphere of darkness
her silver embrace.

I woke before sunrise; something significant had roused me to consciousness. The darkness of my room was interlaced with light. I knew immediately what it was; it has happened many times before. I opened the curtains dreamily, yet energised by this captivating magic.

Moonlight always strikes me as incredibly, even improbably, powerful; and yet paradoxically soft, beguiling, yielding. It possesses a wholly different quality to the garish light of the sun. It is the sun's nocturnal complement, delicately silky, elusive, opalescent, yin, like the visual equivalent of a lullaby. And, I am convinced, it encapsulates a living, pulsating spirit of its own which goes way beyond the remit of physics. (It is an interesting paradox to me that, although the moon exerts gravity, I prefer to think of its mercurial nature, its inexpressibly light touch, its delicacy and spiritual magnetism.)

Sunlight is essential for life on earth; that is a truism. And the sun rising over mountains, setting over the sea, has a transcendent beauty of its own which attracts countless worshippers. I appreciate that and share in it. But I remain a devotee of the moon, a lunar celebrant. Perhaps even a benign lunatic!

As a Piscean I love water; I love seeing breakers crashing onto a beach; I am mesmerised by the glint of moonlight on the sea, as though the planet itself were shattering into millions of fragments and reassembling aloft in the sky, where it retains its form, its integrity, its 'enso' or perfect circle, its benign expression (yes, look closely; there really is a face!), and its seductive allure. And in the same way that the moon's gravity controls the movements of the oceans, so it clandestinely and gnomically affects the energies of my body and soul. I feel that I too ebb and flow under its regenerative influence.

I gaze up through slightly parted curtains, peeping like an innocent full of wonder, whisked back into the unadulterated world of childhood, and I am enchanted by that nacreous orb, that perfect form. That physical and yet symbolic presence illuminated our ancestors in the very same way through countless generations: long dead eyes would once have seen precisely the same visions that we see. There is the link: the moon as connection, as a bowl of light blessing every human, every animal, every living thing and, yes, every mountain, lake and desert, gentled beneath its nocturnal benediction. Blessing, over time, our forbears, forging a link.

It is the pristine reflection of the full moon that means so much, that moves the heart, that filters through the body and energises the spirit; that gives such joy to those who would, as it were, meet it half way. It feels timeless, its light emanating from a sacred mystery, not simply the sun; the one source, the beginning of all things – if indeed there was a beginning.

The circularity of the full moon symbolises perfection and purity, I always feel, and functions as a metaphor for time. Time may be perceived as linear, the historian's view, which accords with most people's perception; or circular, as evidenced by the seasons and cosmic revolutions. Perhaps it is both. Perhaps all time exists in a moment – this moment. Perhaps it is nothing more than change.

I think of the seasons; the revolutions of the earth itself; birth and death and rebirth; the Wheel of the Year, central to the lives of farmers, pagans, spiritual seekers; labyrinths with their peripheral starting points and intense energies at their centres; the circles of sacred Neolithic sites, of pagan gatherings, of the ceremonies of indigenous peoples, often conducted under the auspices of the moon.

Unlike many, I was not excited by the first moon landing; I was saddened, rather. I view the footsteps of humans on the moon as a desecration. We have negligently spoilt so much of the beautiful earth that to move on to the moon in our restless spirit of 'conquest', our search for 'knowledge' (which really means scientific rather than esoteric knowledge) seemed to me a huge mistake, a kind of blasphemy, if you will. Some things we should leave alone.

Physical exploration of the moon will tend to remove, or at least dilute, its magic, its charm, its soul, and risks turning it into another commodity ripe for exploitation and international conflict. I want to immerse myself in the abiding mystery of the moon from the vantage point of earth, not analyse it and demystify it.

Perhaps I am hopelessly idealistic, too ethereal, hypersensitive to that especial lunar light. But I know that others approach the moon from a position of faith rather than rationality and, as with landscapes of the earth, encourage the preservation of wilderness. In great numbers, human footprints tend to ruin.

I rather like the idea of the cosmic wilderness, untouched by human hand but celebrated by the human spirit. In celestial terms the moon is incredibly close to us, and thus so vulnerable. To view it from afar, albeit with some esoteric connection, is to respect it as a close member of what Native Americans would call 'Father Sky' (complementing 'Mother Earth').

And, thinking of Native Americans, a lovely, edifying story comes to mind.

A team of astronauts training for the first moon landing in 1969 were stationed in a remote, moon-like desert in the southwestern USA. An old Native American came across them and asked what they were doing. 'Training to land on the moon,' they replied. The old Native American fell silent, then said, 'I wonder if you could do me a favour?' 'What might that be?' they asked. 'Well,' said the old man, 'the people of my tribe believe that holy spirits live on the moon. I was wondering if you could pass on an important message to them from my people.' 'What's the message?' said the astronauts. The old man muttered some words in his tribal language and asked the astronauts to repeat it again and again until they had memorised it. 'What does this message mean?' the astronauts asked. 'Oh, I can't tell you. It's a secret that only our tribe and the moon spirits are allowed to know.'

Returning to base after the historic moon landing, the astronauts found someone who spoke the old man's tribal language and asked her to translate the secret message. After reiterating the message in a language the astronauts clearly did not understand, the translator burst into uncontrollable laughter.

'What's so funny?' the astronauts asked, somewhat peeved. The translator explained that the carefully memorised sentence meant, 'Don't believe a single word these people are telling you. They have come to steal your land.'

I had to laugh to myself. I think that this is a particularly revealing allegory.

I draw, paint and meditate on the full moon. Such practices, combined with others, keep me grounded. Although I greatly appreciate a half moon, a gibbous moon and that exquisite ghostly slither of the new moon, it is the full moon, sitting on the sea or peeping from behind a mountain, or simply hanging there wondrous in a starlit sky, that totally satisfies my need for connection. It is a pearl of great value, yet open to all.

I am a lunar child through and through.

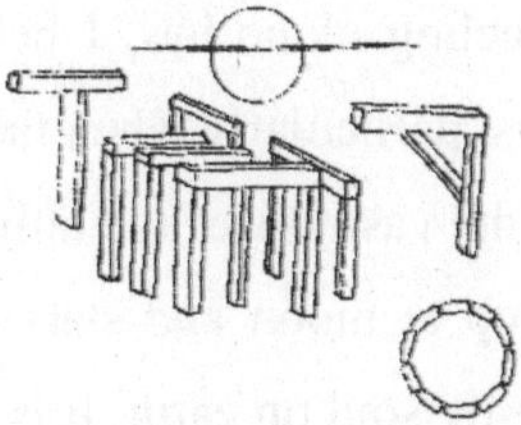

8 ANCESTRAL VOICES

The far-sounding bell
calls to the heart of this world,
speaks of another.

'The ancients make their presence delightful.'

NAVAJO

This is the starting point.

It is all too easy to feel alone, abandoned or disconnected; but, despite appearances, you are never really any of those. Not if heart and mind are open, and not if you can make yourself subtly perceptive. I think that it is often a question of tuning in, of wavelength. Isolation, alienation, disconnection, abandonment – call it what you will – seems like a peculiarly modern curse. It isn't. The sense of feeling alone has, I believe, always existed amongst human beings, particularly when faced with our apparent insignificance within the vastness of the universe.

I too have gazed up at moon and stars on a clear night and felt.... well, like the only soul on earth. It is of course a delusion, but a powerful one. Modern life, with its global communications, its spurious ease of connection and its instant multitude of 'friends', can paradoxically increase one's sense of isolation; for to connect with someone else's voice or image is not really to be with them in the fullest, most authentic sense.

We need physical proximity as well as spiritual alignment; actual embrace to deepen remote exchanges of ideas and sentiments; the flesh and blood and eye contact of another, their breath and fragrance, to be fulfilled.

But there is quite a different sense in which one may be able to connect, to celebrate union and harmony with others; something which goes way beyond modern forms of communication and physical proximity. This involves a deep and abiding awareness of ancestors; a sensitivity to the spirits which evolve over time – often many thousands of years – and affect us here and now. It also involves an acknowledgement of sages, philosophers and spiritual teachers.

Buddhism teaches us to 'live in the moment', that only the here and now really exist. I have a great deal of respect for that view – I am attracted to Buddhism of the peculiar Zen tradition – but it is not the whole story and sidelines, if not entirely ignores, a very important element within the human psyche: namely memory. Not only individual memory – yours and mine – which persists for a single lifetime; but more particularly what might be called 'folk memory' or 'ancestor awareness'. Lao Tzu and Buddha speak to us still, in a certain impalpable sense.

All those places I have visited – forests, mountains, oceans, churches, temples, shrines, Neolithic sites and magical gardens – all resonate with the spirits of those who came before, often long before. In one sense nothing is ever lost, only reformulated. One senses the presence of the dead as living still in the collective memory, but perhaps at times even more tangibly than that.

All is in flux, and time itself may constitute an illusion: is it linear, cyclical or both? Can what is ostensibly dead ever return or, more powerfully, remain with us on a different plane? It is a fascinating conundrum: death begetting more life.

Every rose whose fragrance delights me possesses the essence of roses which grew over thousands of years. Every butterfly whose patterns I marvel at honours countless generations of butterflies receding in time. Every tree leaf I touch takes me back to the original virgin forest in the mystical beginning. Every child in whose eyes I see innocence contains multitudes of her innocent ancestors. Everything is lost and yet, transformed, everything remains. It is an exquisite paradox.

Dylan Thomas tells us, 'The force that through the green fuse drives the flower drives my green age.' What is the nature of that force? I would suggest that it is a mystery, it is energy unsusceptible to scientific investigation – this life-force, this thrilling and ubiquitous energy – that touches us even when we are unaware of it.

Taoism teaches the interconnectedness, the unity, the harmony of all things in the universe, not merely matter but also spirit, and not only in space but in time. The Tao is the way of all things, an essence which is beyond the meagre power of human language to articulate. Some things are felt, understood by the body and the heart, but cannot be captured in language. Our fugitive, elusive connection with the ancients is like that. Buddha enjoins us to listen with the heart and be still and in stillness all will be understood. Take time out of the stream of endless chatter.

I recall as a small boy being taken to the British Museum, to the Egyptian Room, and there, in a glass case, I saw the sand-preserved body, in a touchingly foetal position, of a man who evidently died three thousand years ago. Three thousand! I stared, fascinated but also mystified, for a long time. How could this be?

The dead decompose, don't they? Not this man. He still possessed teeth, a rictus, and I could reconstruct his face in imagination. He should have utterly vanished, forgotten forever; but there he was, an ancestor of someone alive now, perhaps of many of us. As an impressionable boy the hairs prickled on my neck.

I recall wondering, in my naïve way, whether the dead can live again, whether indeed there is a resurrection, if not of the flesh then of the spirit. That Egyptian mummy did not smell of fragrant roses nor, encased, of anything. But he deserves to be remembered as a representative of us all: the flight of a butterfly through time; a leaf's millennial self-replication; the innocent gaze of a newborn endlessly repeated in the cycle of living and dying and living once again. Discover great joy in that – in not being alone.

When I hear the wind in the trees, what it is that I am perhaps subliminally hearing are the voices of all those people who came before me, driving my green age. The song, part lament, part hymn, part joyful rhapsody, of ancestors.

9 PAYING ATTENTION

Look closely, marvel
at rainbows in the wings of
silken butterflies.

I was walking through the garden alone. But I was not really alone. As I trod a sinuous path, stepping as lightly as I could, I quickly became aware of the abundance of life either side of me. This was not any garden, but one imbued with a particular spirit, a kind of lovingkindness which had clearly accumulated and distilled over years of heartfelt visitations; the essences, one might say, of many people.

Those people, those garden celebrants, had gone before me and had paved the way for my presence there. I felt truly honoured and grateful for this place and became aware, through mindful movement, and a kind of soft, liminal focussing, of my invisible but all too real companions. The validity of my experience owed everything to the unforced but meticulous paying of attention, the awakening of spiritual awareness.

I had watched other people, not in this garden but in similar natural surroundings, and had noticed a scattered attention, or perhaps some sore distraction. But why? Well, in some cases, it seemed to me, based on close observation of body language and vacant expression, these walkers were absorbed in some remote matter, some thorny issue which prevented connection with the living presence around them in the garden, or in the woods or fields they travelled.

In other cases the individuals lacked authentic presence as a result of their focus, to the exclusion of everything else, on electronic devices: smartphone screens or personal music players. Whatever the distraction, their attention drifted from these surroundings and this moment to some other place and time. Buddha said simply be here, now; that is the only way to connect, the only way to be.

It saddens me greatly when people overlook the physical beauty all around them: beside the garden path, within the trees, along the seashore, high above in the mountains and the configurations of cloud. All these in addition to the more subtle spiritual presences.

Modern life, separating us from our roots, tends to do this increasingly and, writ large, diminishes people's sensitivity to the degradation of the earth which results from habitually failing to pay sufficient attention. Whatever we fail to notice, or wholly ignore, will eventually suffer. Our general neglect is a death knell.

I recall that garden with quiet joy; it lives not merely in the memory but in my soul. But my recollections are not only of the visual and aesthetic aspects; running deeper is a numinous connection, an ever-presence inside me, of the vital reality of that place.

I felt utterly at peace whilst treading the interlinking paths and crossing the sloping lawns and skirting the route of the holy and salubrious watercourse. All of this lives in me now because I was paying attention then. I gloried in the moment-by-moment experience of the garden and welcomed every colour, contour, texture and fragrance of it into my being. As a result, a kind of resonance, an imprint, of that place stays within me.

I needed no photographs; they would have been yet another

distraction, glib and too easy to accomplish. I have a composite image sketched in my mind, a mental photograph and the imperfect archive of my sketchbook. Both will go when I go; the garden will remain for other apostles.

Those who walked the same paths before me will know exactly what I mean. I am linked to them because we are all connected to the astounding, life-enhancing garden.

I recall consciously walking very slowly but without undue effort – tai chi walking, moving meditation – willing my mind to notice every leaf, every bloom, every butterfly, every trickle of water and every trick of sunlight. I took time out to sit and draw trees and, as I did so, sensed the trees giving me something back as I graced them in a humble and unobtrusive fashion.

I would suggest that garden ramblers, and beachcombers and woodland walkers for that matter, pocket their gadgets (yes, and even their sketchbooks!) and, unmediated, pay unconditional attention to the breath, the essence, the wind on their skin, the bees and butterflies crossing their paths, the heart of the matter.

Only then will a sense of the sacred generate the silent utterance of a prayer, a thanksgiving for the astounding mystery which enfolds and sanctifies us.

10 THE SPIRIT OF TREES

In the dark forest
a berry drops through branches:
sound of leaves breathing.

Whenever I feel in need of rejuvenation I take a stroll through woodland. It doesn't take long for the magic to work. The sensations I feel are essentially beyond words; language is inadequate, and yet always there arises an impulse to explain, to rationalise, to put into context, the power of trees.

Trees can transform us, if only we allow them in their bewitching repose and near silence to work their enchantment upon us. For trees act as an unwitting antidote to the often bleak angular and mechanical landscapes of modern life. We need them, we need more and more of them – from the colossal sequoias to the diminutive bonsai – but globally we have sacrificed so many and we lose more every day: they are mistakenly regarded as expendable commodities. Logging is not living, except for a few.

I recognise a contradiction here: I love books, and books are trees transmuted into things of a very different potency. The physical rootedness of trees mirrors and symbolises my own desire for rootedness. Sometimes I feel oddly disconnected from the earth, cast adrift, the anchor of my soul uprooted. I struggle in the ocean of day-to-day concerns, desperately treading water.

And then as therapy and relief I wander through an avenue of oaks, a stand of beeches, and something vital, unfathomable, returns to me. Some ancestral voice calls through the interstices of breeze and branch and I begin to feel whole again; I begin to sense a restoration of belonging, a renewed commitment, a rapt association. The process of healing begins.

There is clearly an evolutionary, subconscious awareness at work here, a link to forest-dwelling ancestors, rooted in the folk psyche. All humans owe a debt of gratitude to distant ancestors for their intimate connection to the land, the immemorial rhythms of their lives which find a distant echo or resonance over time in our own twenty-first century existence. Atavism is a very real and valuable thing, but it has been weakened by the alienating effects of technological civilisation.

Trees can bring us back to an awareness of who we really are and where we came from and what, after all, we are still viscerally attached to. Trees are like some verdant umbilical cord.

When I sit in the midst of woodland I sense a sacredness in the air, the presence of an intangible divinity; an ineffable catharsis. The tree canopy creates a kind of al fresco cathedral around me, a holy space, a shrine, a pagan sanctuary. In close observation of leaf, branch and flower I feel cleansed and uplifted, as though those far distant ancestors are working through me, their spirits experiencing a resurrection through the medium of the tree and inviting me into their circle.

Trees are solid, palpable, flexible, dynamic living things; and yet they can be elusive, fugitive, fluid, numinous beings, standing apart yet intimately connected to us and to each other. They weave around us. They come and go, rise and fall, are subjected to felling and fire; but still there is something changeless about them: the tree of life with its myriad branches which, when pruned, will grow again and will flourish even in hardship. They map our existence.

Forests and woodlands provide an escape from the mundane,

the workaday, the artificial angles and non-organic materials of the urban landscape. Trees soften a city's environment, emphasising the importance of parks and tree-lined avenues in what would otherwise be arid spaces. In cities trees would be 'noticed' even more keenly if they were not present!

Some years ago I took to growing bonsai, collecting seeds whenever and wherever I could, drying them, storing them until what I considered a propitious moment. Then I would sow them and pray that they would reward me with their unobtrusive life, their enchantment and generosity of germination.

With most I was not disappointed. In the main I prefer trees to grow wild, naturally, uncultivated, unpruned, unfettered, remote from plantations with their serried ranks; and thus my bonsai saddened me as well as delighted me. For I realise that in miniaturising them, in establishing strict control, I stunted their growth and greatly reduced their magnificence. Trees need freedom too.

But I like to think that I have nurtured seed that might otherwise have fallen on stony ground; a small, mindful act of rescue, perhaps, the creation of tiny living icons and a world in miniature.

Trees provide a rich and abundant habitat for so many living things, from birds to insects, from fungi to lichen and, yes, mistletoe. And such largesse also provides human beings with a superabundance of elegance and splendour; an awareness of the intimate relationship of all things. Trees are complex webs of life, matrices of vibrancy and regeneration, loci of wonder and grace.

I walk amongst trees and, silently, deep in my soul, unforced and unguarded, express gratitude for the presence of these rooted, balanced, and earth-nourishing companions.

Cathedrals are tributes to God and human ingenuity; trees are tributes to the mysterious sanctity which pervades all natural landscapes.

If, in an increasingly indoor, disconnected existence, we ignore the therapeutic and immemorial significance of woodlands, we do so at our peril. Spirits are all around us, as indigenous peoples know full well; but the spirit of trees whispers a liminal windblown mantra which, for those willing to listen, creates a lifetime of enchantment.

11 MANDALA BENEATH ANCIENT YEWS

Build the monastery,
grow the trees. Yet in a flash
all traces vanish.

The guardian yews spread right across the lower reaches of the garden, alongside the healing stream which trickles down from the holy well. Beneath the yews two Tibetan monks have erected a vivid and resplendent yurt. The low-sweeping branches of the yews seem both to protect and complement the yurt, the trees' leaves deep green verging into black, the yurt by contrast a swirling rainbow bedecked with flags and ribbons.

I have never before seen a yurt in this familiar garden; I have never seen shaven-headed, saffron-and-burgundy robed monks here either. For an entire week this magical retreat is transformed into a makeshift Buddhist monastery, complete with the most evocative chanting and peals of bells and rhythmic drumming which at times bedazzle the senses. The inbetween silences become even more resoundingly silent in contrast to the spiritual resonance which beguiles heart and mind and soothes the senses. For a while this place seems like the centre of the world.

I enter the yurt to find half a dozen intrigued visitors standing or sitting on cushions. They face two monks, who sit cross-legged close to a large, low table in the centre which is reminiscent of a square dais. By their sides the monks have access to open dishes of fine sand in a bewildering range of vivid colours.

They have begun the process of creating a mandala. It will 'consume' them – I use the word advisedly – for the entire week. They will labour for eight hours a day, sometimes longer, crouched over the table, with few breaks inbetween.

I watch for half an hour, fascinated by the absolute concentration of the monks, who allow no distraction. I am told that, throughout each day, they will only occasionally eat and drink and take exercise.Their devotion to the task is total and I'm sure would shame most Westerners who paint or write or engage in craftwork, or birdwatch or indulge in any other pursuit which might be called obsessive. What these singular devotees undertake requires huge single-mindedness, not to say a kind of touching gentleness and delicacy.

There is a profound purpose to this construction of an elaborate, intricate and surpassingly beautiful mandala, which I shall come to.

For the moment, beneath the enfolding arms of the guardian yews, the two Tibetan monks, using funnels which resemble inverted delicate ice cream cones, sprinkle powdery sand – violet, ochre, ultramarine, emerald, scarlet, black, white, every rainbow shade and more – with meticulous care onto a template of tiny squares, crescents, rectangles, circles, stars and needle-thin lines, thus fashioning a kaleidoscopic image.

It is a kind of two-dimensional representation of a temple. Lifted and stretched into the space above the table, if such a thing were possible, it would produce a multi-coloured temple for the most diminutive of monks.

These men know what they are doing, although the non-monastic audience, myself included, seem a little bemused if full of admiration for their unstinting application and pinpoint accuracy. These monks have engaged on a mental marathon on each of the seven days of this week. But to what purpose?

Well, the mandala itself represents a number of interlinked ideas incorporated into a traditional structure consisting of a circle enclosing a square with a deity on each of its four sides. The entire mandala is meant to symbolise the universe. It is a template for everything that exists, expressed in diagrammatic form. It is sacred, iconic, revered – and designed to convey the Buddhist concept of impermanence.

I walk the garden up to the holy well, on slightly higher ground than the lawn on which the guardian yews stand with the yurt nestled between them. I sit by the well and close my eyes and contemplate the notion of impermanence, the ephemerality of all things. Whilst doing this I am conscious of the eventual fate of the Tibetan monks' exquisite mandala, which is still in the making. It seems strange yet apposite.

The next day I visit the yurt and once again, standing in a rapt circle of visitors, marvel at the monks' supreme dedication. They sit one either side of the partially completed mandala. They dip their little funnels into carefully selected dishes of sand – precisely the right shade of blue or green or red or yellow – and proceed to fill another tiny geometrical shape. They keep a subtle watch on each other's work, working in unison, with one mind, as it were.

I lean over the shoulder of one monk, feeling a little obtrusive, in order to observe the exquisite fineness of a long straight line he is making with black sand. It is almost like embroidery, as if, using tiny grains instead of stitches, he is joining together the geometrical shapes beneath him – beneath all of us – there in the breath-held confines of the yurt.

The monks occasionally adjust their robes over the shoulder or across the knees; occasionally stretch out an otherwise folded-up leg; arch their necks which must, surely, after so many almost motionless hours, be aching. They show no signs of flagging, their faces expressionless, except in odd moments of recognition, one might say human connection.

One of the monks darts a look at some young children who sit cross-legged on the matted flooring and appear utterly absorbed, perhaps bemused, by this strange process, this esoteric endeavour. The monk briefly and enigmatically smiles at the children, conveying a moment of gentle recognition, almost of tenderness.

I leave the yurt once more and take a long walk around the gardens and out into the countryside. When I observe the landscape panoramically, breathing deeply because my breath is my life, the wind that blows through me, and some of the oxygen I inhale must be exhaled by the ranks of woodlands before me; I realise that one day none of this – myself included – will exist in anything like its present form.

All, however beautiful, however precious, is subject to change and dissolution. All will be absorbed into the cosmos and transmuted into… what? Not gold, certainly, but something that engenders clean, fresh growth; a new consciousness; perhaps some future forms unimaginable to us.

On the seventh day I return to the yurt – the Tibetan monks haven't rested ! The mandala is complete, the circle, the square, the deities, the spectacular colours, the minute detail, the stunning perfection. It has taken two monks over fifty hours of eye-straining, back-breaking labour. We stand and admire them and their unique artistry. One monk exhales audibly.

And then, at a nod, the monks place their hands flat on the fragile, vivid segments of the mandala and scatter the sand into a kind of grainy, swirling soup, like a multi-coloured beach that the tide has overwhelmed. It has been destroyed at a stroke! A week's devoted labour! Quite deliberately, with prayers and forethought.

Some of us appear shocked, even though I think we all knew what was coming – except perhaps the young children. As though we had witnessed Michelangelo taking a sledgehammer to the just completed statue of David. Or Monet slicing through the canvas of his waterlilies. Perhaps I exaggerate wildly – but there is a parallel.

The point of this entire painstaking exercise is designed to convey the Buddhist concept of impermanence: however beautiful an object may be, however invaluable, however exquisite an emotion, everything is subject to change.

The two monks smile broadly, even mischievously, at each other and at us, dumbfounded as we are, then bow slowly and reverentially.

I step outside the yurt feeling peculiarly moved, if a little disconcerted. One might even say enlightened. It has taken an entire week of ceaseless toil and dedication.

I am glad that the guardian yews still stand resolutely above us, still stretch out their arms protectively. I wonder how long they will remain?

12 ROBIN AT THE BLOOD SPRING

Bright angel, alive,
lit by the flame of your wings,
one in love's circle.

I sat on a bench by the Vesica Pool in glorious sunshine. Others were sitting on the lawn which sloped down to the pool, or simply wandering. This place entranced me. I sat eating some bread, cheese and nuts, simple fare, supposedly the poet's breakfast. I felt at ease with the world, preternaturally relaxed. It produces an exquisite feeling when time seems to stand still; when the worries of the world are cast, at least for a time, into the background; when all that exists is this place and this moment.

I thought of the sacred well which sits at the top of the enchanted garden in the shade of interwoven trees which surround the wellhead and form a protective, shrine-like canopy. I reflected on the waters themselves, which flow rust-red and iron-rich, a chalybeate blessing which visitors sip for the healing qualities. Everything about this place radiates health and invites prolonged contemplation.

I sat nibbling my bread, cheese and nuts and tilted my head back to absorb the warmth and benediction of the sun. I felt my very consciousness change in a way that is essentially indescribable, but clearly occurs in such moments. It is a Zen truism that we cannot use words to capture the deepest feelings.

As my awareness drifted, perceptions modified. I became sensitive to people's voices taking on a distant, dreamlike quality. I felt unusually light, as though I might float above the bench, the garden, the town itself. All this was subjective – or was it? What is it that anchors us and then in flight sets us free?

A sharp chirping very close by brought me back to this place and this moment; to mundane consciousness. The sound was sweet, brittle but insistent. I opened my eyes and gazed at the ground by my feet.

A robin stood cheekily looking up at me, its head cocked to one side. Every few moments it called in such a penetrating voice for such a tiny bird. I was charmed, intrigued, delighted by such fearlessness, such presence, such chutzpah.

On the wooden slats of the bench sat the remainder of my

bread, cheese and nuts. The crinkled, flattened paper bag acted as a plate. I sensed some almost telepathic connection with the robin, its determined appeal: it was as peckish as I had been.

I picked up a crust of bread and crumbled it and placed some of the crumbs on the open palm of my hand. I held my hand low to the ground, close to the robin, which immediately, disarmingly, skipped onto my palm, pecked up a few crumbs and then darted away at lightning speed. I was astonished at this wild bird's friendliness.

I knew from digging in my own garden how amiable such birds can be. Many is the time I have shoved the digging fork upright in the soil, only to see an opportunistic robin perch upon it boldly if briefly a few feet from where I stood. But I had never had such a creature alight on my hand. Such close proximity was, to me, unheard of.

I gazed around the Vesica Pool from my seated vantage point. The robin had vanished. It had taken a few crumbs from me and abandoned our all too brief connection.

Then I caught sight of it again, sitting in a bush singing its heart out as if serenading me, repaying me for the largesse of crumbs. I smiled to myself, knowing what a fanciful notion this was; how we sometimes wilfully imagine what is not real; how we anthropomorphise creatures whose lives are very different from our own.

Later that day I came across a passing gardener and told him of my encounter with the robin. He smiled knowingly.

"Oh, that's our tame robin. She knows everybody here. Fearless. Cheeky. Opportunistic, of course."

"Of course. She took some breadcrumbs right out of my hand."

"You're lucky she didn't take your heart and soul as well."

"Pardon?"

"Many people have come here to the garden and spoken about the robin. She is often seen up at the wellhead where people meditate."

"Does she sing loudly up there, too?"

"No, she is silent. She seems – absurd notion, I know – to understand the demands of silence."

"What do you call her?"

"Robin."

"Just that?"

"Just that." He smiled again. "She's the archetypal robin."

I didn't know whether or not to believe the gardener. I wanted to, but logic and rationality persuaded me that robins, like other birds, do not behave with such awareness of human desires. Or do they?

I went up to the wellhead, which is at the opposite end of the garden from the Vesica Pool, on higher ground and more enclosed. I sat on the low stone wall which circles the great iron cover of the well, which is always propped open.

I thought of the red-tinged waters, which I had often sipped; I visualised the robin's breast, which is not nearly as bright and lurid as depicted in Christmas cards but a somewhat subtler, rustier colour.

For some reason I remembered the blood of Christ, the holy wine brimming in a chalice, the wafers of bread offered for healing and redemption. All of these things seemed to overwhelm me in one epiphanic image. But what had these things to do with a single bird?

When I returned to the Vesica Pool I sat, not on the bench, but on the steep slope of lawn which runs down to the pool on the opposite side. The robin was nowhere to be seen. I felt somewhat disappointed. Perhaps she was no longer peckish or companionable.

The friendly gardener came by, smiled and waved. I called him over.

"What's happened to the tame robin?"

"Nothing. She comes and goes like some elusive magus."

"Magus? What do you mean?"

"She's a real talking point in the gardens. She seems in some strange, unfathomable way to unite people, to enchant them, the way she darts about, the way she blesses us with her brilliance and her cheeky importuning."

The gardener walked on, smiling to himself. I had never thought of a robin, or of any bird, in that way. That sharp, penetrative, distinctive chirping seemed to fill my head when I retired to bed that night in the retreat house which nestled in the lower reaches of the garden. I couldn't tell if I actually heard the robin herself or some phantasmal distant echo of the tiny creature. It didn't matter.

In slanting moonlight I glanced at my open palm, the one on which the robin had fleetingly perched. Right in the middle was a faint red mark. I glanced at my other palm, just to check: an identical red mark. Like two stigmata. I thought so.

One way or another I was changed. I would never consume the poet's breakfast of bread, cheese and nuts in quite the same way again. What I had sacrificed was little enough; what I had gained was a whole new understanding.

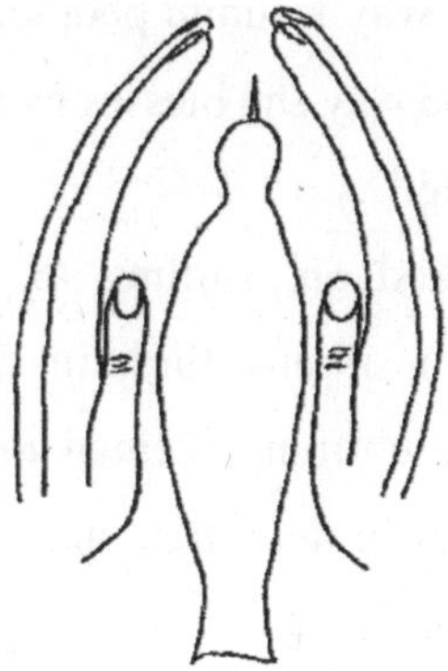

13 A DOVE COLLARED

Fine axis of life
spun, strained, taut to breaking point:
outstretched, love's thread holds.

I was about to walk from the house across the lawn to the end of the garden, which takes me past the birdtable. Usually there are all manner of birds fluttering around it, from tiny, exquisitely coloured blue tits, darting flashes of light, to the occasional stentorian, dive-bombing seagull. That morning the birdtable was deserted, although I had been careful, as always, to load it with mixed seeds. But there was something on the lawn which caught my eye and intrigued me.

I saw a bird completely motionless, hunched up, sitting in the centre of the lawn. It was highly unusual because this particular bird was clearly not roosting. It was not in the big cedar tree which overcanopies the lawn, nor was it lodged in some secluded, protective hideaway. It was not feeding and, if one of a pair, its partner was nowhere to be seen. I thought that perhaps it was badly injured, or sick, biding its time out there in a completely exposed area of the garden, clearly indifferent to prowling cats. Perhaps slowly fading away.

The thought struck me that this resting or ailing or semi-comatose avian occupied almost the same spot on my lawn where, six summers before, I had discovered a deceased Red Admiral in perfect condition. Was this square yard of lawn some kind of Bermuda Triangle in miniature, zapping aerial creatures instead of high-flying aircraft? This notion, fleeting as it was, seemed somewhat fanciful, to say the least.

But a bird was there, inert, facing down the garden, unwilling or unable to move, and clearly unaware of my presence. From the rear it resembled a small, uniformly pale-grey pigeon. But it was not a pigeon, not quite. A late addition to the pigeon order, 'Streptopelia decaocto' is more delicate and, one might argue, refined. If that is what it was.

At first, from a distance of thirty feet, I could not positively identify it; all I had was a hunch. I walked slowly towards the bird, closing to about twenty feet. As its head turned slightly, I stopped. We were both utterly silent, statue-like, even comical. But I daren't laugh.

Then I took even slower steps, indulged in a little tai chi walking, and crept up on this unsuspecting creature. I meant it no harm, of course; I am neither hunter nor predator. Rather, I was deeply curious, and as always my one desire was to reaffirm my connection with creatures of the wild and the earth itself.

I closed to within ten feet of the motionless bird. Its head turned slightly once more. I halted, stilled myself, crouched lower over the grass, concentrating intensely. I could see one eye of the bird, and I was sure it caught sight of me – but it did not budge an inch, except that subtle half-turn of the head. It was squat and fat and stoical – a Buddha bird!

Creeping up, I could see at last that this creature was indeed Streptopelia decaocto – a collared dove. I have seen pairs of them in the garden, usually fluttering onto the pitched roof of the birdtable, sometimes pecking up seed from the lawn, sometimes dancing a kind of tarantella. They are half the size of their bullish cousins, wood pigeons, more delicate, a softer shade of grey, and display that touching white ruff.

I came to within two feet of the bird. It amazed me that it made no attempt to move and seemed, incredibly, unaware of my close proximity. I crouched low, just behind the dove, extended an arm, held out an index finger and stroked the bird gently down its back, just once. I felt its warmth, its downy softness, if not quite its heartbeat.

Sensing my touch, the collared dove immediately took flight, strongly, purposefully, and gained altitude as it planed the air above the boundary fence and peeled off to the right. Clearly there had been nothing wrong with it, so swiftly and with such vigour did it move.

I was left wondering. For a few moments I pondered on an important point: had I invaded the collared dove's privacy, startled her, committed some kind of obscure minor transgression?

When I gazed at the spot where the dove had sat heavily, like a little grey bundle of flesh and bone, I caught sight of a tiny, whitish, insubstantial feather. The collared dove had left a scintilla of its physical self behind – and, in addition, a treasured memory.

I picked up the feather, which was little more than a piece of fluff, and placed it in the palm of my hand – exactly as I had done with the Red Admiral six summers before – and entered my study. I placed the little feather on a shelf by my desk, where it remains to this day; a gentle, ghostly reminder of a strange but illuminating encounter.

Later that day I refilled the birdtable with seed, assuming that the collared dove would at some time return, perhaps with its partner, and remind me of the day I had succeeded in getting close enough to stroke its back and establish some sort of connection.

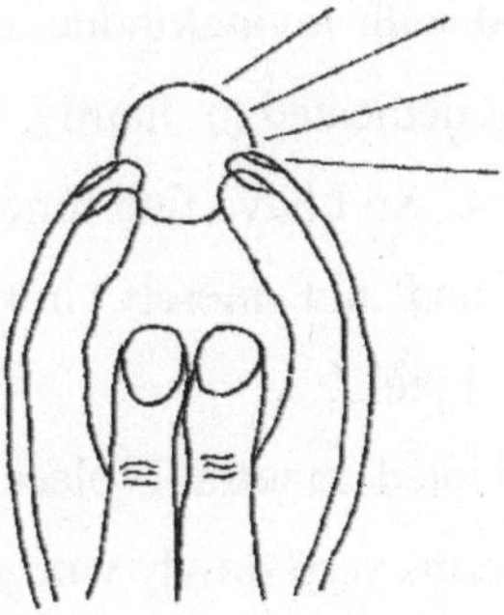

14 PLACING THE PALMS

Prayer? A waking heart,
activity of stillness,
live inter-presence.

Each morning, following my tai chi practice, I stand upright and motionless and recite a prayer to myself. It goes like this: 'May I be filled with lovingkindness, may I be well. May I be peaceful and at ease, may I be happy.' Not an original mantra of mine, but gleaned from a book of spiritual practices.

I follow this very brief prayer, which a long time ago struck me as perhaps a little egoistic – 'May *I* be filled… may *I* be well…' – with a crucial variation.

'May *you* be filled with lovingkindness, may *you* be well...' and so on. The '*you*' is dedicated to 'family, friends, acquaintances and all living creatures.' So I have fine-tuned the prayer to send it outwards to others and not merely inwards to myself. An important distinction, I feel.

Following the adapted mantra I place my upraised palms together, moving my arms very slowly with great deliberation, and touch my lips lightly with kissing thumbs. Then I bow slightly. And then the daily practice is complete and I feel grounded.

It occurred to me some time ago that, in a very tactile sense, the touching of one palm against the other, the equal and mirrored touching of fingers and thumbs, was not only a spiritual act but an exquisite bodily one too.

How many people place their palms together at face level, in silence, with reverence, and luxuriate in the pure physical sensation, the warmth and quiet joy that that creates?

In Asian countries, bringing the palms together before the face indicates greeting, gratitude, parting, reverence, a kind of soft submission to the presence of whatever transcendent being such believers wish to show their devotion to. Similarly, in the Christian tradition, placing the palms lightly together precedes prayer and contemplation of perhaps an ostensibly different almighty, although it seems to me that God, Mohammed, Krishna, Buddha, the Creator and pagan deities, for that matter, are really self-chosen labels for one and the same entity: the source of all things. The abiding mystery. Creation itself, if indeed there ever was such an original event.

The slow, tactile, mindful placing of one open hand against the other demonstrates many things: time out from the sometimes manic swirl of life; personal commitment to the soul, the spirit, the inner being and the outer reality; a renewed desire for connection; a pointing of the way; an acknowledgement of the flesh, the quick of nerves, the pulse of a single human body which reverberates through the universe; a simple act of kindness and devotion.

Each morning prayer and practice are interwoven in the same way. Each morning is like a rebirth, another revolution and a resurrection. The placing of palms seems somehow, in one simple, private, unobtrusive act, a distillation of the essence of everything worthy and true.

May you be well…

15 A HABIT OF BLACK SWANS

Three angels, alive,
lit by the flame of their wings,
one in love's circle.

I stayed in the monastery on retreat, the first time at this particular holy place. But I very soon began to wonder how holy it really was. A monastery with a National Trust-style giftshop, a self-service café, coachloads of visitors and slick advertising everywhere doesn't inspire confidence – not in this penitent, anyway. I was anticipating something more understated, more restrained, more authentic, more old-fashioned, even.

But the modern world, with its insistent commercialism and rapid connectivity must, I suppose, infiltrate even the holiest of places. It was billed as a functioning Franciscan monastery, with time-weathered buildings and beautiful grounds. A picturesque river skirted one boundary and offered superb views over lush countryside. There were outdoor shrines at every turn.

I arrived, signed in at what felt like hotel reception, and was led to a room in a magnificent stretch of medieval buildings, which must have contained at least a dozen ground floor rooms, or 'cells', and many more upstairs and in the roofspace. These buildings faced a grass quadrangle surrounded by even more three-storey high ancient edifices. In the thirteenth-century these must have counted as high-rise.

The sight was impressive, almost spine-tingling in its sheer visual beauty: the stone, the superabundance of flowering wisteria, the mossy pitched roofs and massive chimneys. And what deepened the impression was the sight, now and then, of brown-robed Franciscan monks casually strolling across the quadrangle, disappearing into arched doorways or venturing further afield into the expansive grounds. This was more like what I had come here for, out of sight of giftshop, café, carpark and advertising: bona fide monks.

My room was tiny: a single bed, a miniscule table, a diminutive corner sink and a hard chair. There were two hooks on the door, for clothes and bags presumably. Nothing else. The window too was tiny, sunk into a two-feet thick stone wall and latticed with black iron. Appropriate, I suppose, for a self-denying monk who has largely renounced worldly possessions and needs only space to sleep, pray and wash (in cold water) and perhaps gaze out of the window into an unattainable world.

I felt peace, despite the conspicuous commercialism. I sensed some mystical connection with the monks of long ago, a succession of whom must have lived in this very cell. Not simply stayed, but lived. Of course the bedroom was modern, as was the table, and the sink could not have been that old. But the unwhitewashed walls, the black timber door with its clunky wooden bolt, impressed me as something immemorial, changeless in a rapidly changing world. Isn't that often what we need, some historical and spiritual constants to hang on to?

Early on my first morning I washed in cold water in the corner sink (cold water to wake me out of slumber and give me the pretence of being masochistically ascetic.) I did not immediately go upstairs to the communal lounge where there were tea-making facilities (the receptionist, very helpful if disappointingly non-monastic, showed me the sparse creature comforts.)

I walked diagonally across the huge grass quadrangle, skirting a wall which seemed composed entirely of flowering wisteria and exuded a heavenly fragrance, and headed for a pond which was just visible beyond a corner gap in the square of buildings.

At that point a Franciscan suddenly appeared from nowhere, as it were, as if he'd emerged miraculously from the stone of the building alongside me. He smiled, nodded, bid me good morning in a surprisingly self-confident, penetrating voice, as if acting the part, and walked by. This brief exchange made me feel oddly welcome.

I stopped and studied him as he went: the capacious long brown habit, the easy stride, the sandals peeping from under the hem of the habit with every movement; the sense that here was a man who perhaps long ago found what he was looking for in life and never looked back. He seemed a world away from the quasi-hotel reception, the coachloads of visitors, the selfie-obsessives and the glossy advertising. He seemed… well, authentically spiritual! As I suppose it should be. It is strange how a simple mantle can convey so much.

I proceeded towards the pond. Before I got near it, I caught sight of another brown-clad Franciscan. He was standing at the very edge of the pond, his sandals almost in the reeds. He held an outsize wooden bowl in the crook of his left arm, and with his right hand scattered what I assume were seeds onto the surrounding grass and across the surface of the pond as far as he could cast them. He was, literally, 'broadcasting'. I was intrigued.

I walked closer to the pond; the monk, his back towards me, was clearly unaware of my presence. I heard him talking very quietly, almost reverentially, to the mallards, moorhens and gulls which swooped at this distribution of manna. He clicked his tongue, this elderly Franciscan, with a touching fondness and a perceptible connection with the birds. And he seemed, bizarrely, to sing in a lilting, hymn-like undertone.

I thought of St Francis and how, down the ages, despite the often stated idea that nothing remains constant – I recall the philosopher Heraclitus's assertion that you can never step in the same river twice – here was living proof that some things, some very human things, do remain constant: a tenderness towards animals, a sublime sensitivity, rituals and ceremonies which defy time. It has been noted before: the actors change but the play remains the same.

I stood and observed from a respectful distance. Out of shadow, for the morning was still in its infancy and bathed in misty half-light, I perceived two ghostly dark shapes. They appeared to glide in tandem over the smooth surface of the pond, which was now peppered with chaff from the monk's seedbowl.

When the shapes solidified, I saw to my astonishment two black swans! I had heard of black swans but never in my life had I actually seen any.

One of the swans waddled onto the muddy margin between grass and water, a few feet to the left of the serenading Fransiscan, stretched its body upright and spread its wings like some dark encompassing angel.

I stood mesmerised. It was as if this particular swan were aware of my surveillance and desired to put on a show of magnificence. Of course, the wing-flapping was not performed for my benefit at all; I was a superfluous bystander.

But those two ebony swans… such a contrast with the usual brilliant whiteness, such exoticism in a thoroughly English setting. They were like rare jewels, living proof of difference, symbols of something I could not quite grasp.

The monk turned away, his seedbowl emptied. At that point he saw me, smiled benignly, bowed his head a little and, without a word, went on his way.

That night, lying in bed in a room which had once been a monk's austere cell, I reflected on the two black swans and the Franciscan brothers whose entire lives are encompassed and defined by this monastery. My enchantment with the swans, indeed my shock at simply seeing them, lingered a long time.

Black swans, brown habits, lilac wisteria, greystone buildings – all changing and yet changeless. All living in the one light.

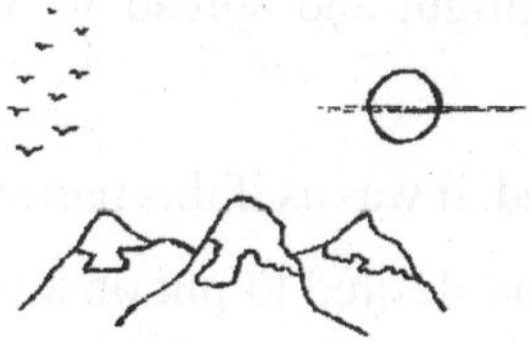

16 SILENCE, STILLNESS, SOLITUDE

First gleam of sunrise;
the shock of recognition;
infinite belief.

I like early morning most of all. I like walking slowly down my garden at dawn or, sometimes, before dawn. I like the mysterious, evocative half-light, shadows created by a resplendent moon. If there is magic in the garden, that is the time to truly experience it. If there is energy, that is when it is at its most potent. If there is truth, not to tell but to feel, the dawning window is the time to appreciate it. There is always a time, always an opportunity for those who are sufficiently sensitive of the need to connect.

Much of modern life militates against mindfulness, connection, groundedness. Intrusive technology has a distancing effect. It is the nature of the way most people live in the twenty-first century, except perhaps the few remaining indigenous peoples who maintain a traditional way of life.

But there are antidotes to the rush-and-tear, and there are subtle therapies for those who become aware, even in a small way, of the immemorial but often suppressed wildness within us. 'Civilised' sometimes means dull, blunted, desensitised. What we need, like all living things, are the most propitious conditions in which to flourish.

Perhaps I might humbly offer some helpful suggestions for the frazzled soul, the sufferer from anxiety and alienation, those disconnected from their essential being. (I have been one.)

First, silence is an almost essential condition, at least for part of each day, for the purpose of replenishing the spiritual batteries. I know that if I stand in my garden early, with the sun coming up, the air calm, no one around but only the company of birds (and maybe the odd fox), I feel amazingly contented; it feels like a homecoming.

Such a beginning to the day is a medicine without unpleasant side-effects; any 'side-effects' are wholly positive. Silence, which of course cannot be absolute, conveys in some ineffable way the essence of the universe. The music of the spheres is absorbed within the greater silence. Communal silence in a holy place has, as most people know, a most powerful and at times overwhelming effect.

What accentuates silence is stillness. These two virtues often, if not always, complement each other, for whatever is truly still is truly silent. I think of clouds, the unruffled surface of a pond, a tree resting free of breezes, a sailing boat becalmed, people meditating, a vase of flowers in an empty room, a church in the held breath before and after the sermon.

When one is still – I mean perfectly still, poised in body and soul without the slightest impulse to act or speak – then one can dissolve into the centre of the self, combining stillness with silence and thus creating a mood of great potency. Energy flows, not with the violence of lightning, but in the sureness of the blood, the pulsations of light, the heat of occult and undemonstrative life.

Many of us crave the company of others and revel in sociability; that is fine, at times essential; that communal feeling, that sharing and mutual support and celebration of human emotions. But aloneness (as distinct from loneliness) and solitude serve important functions too. A spent soul needs gentle recharging,

Alone, at least for a time, I can view my life in a different perspective, without the input or distraction of others. I can test self-reliance, fortitude, resilience, a relaxed love of absent things, and a kind of classic Stoicism inspiringly expressed by such Roman philosophers as Seneca, Epictetus and Marcus Aurelius.

On retreat at several places I know – one a pagan centre, the other a Benedictine abbey, both deeply spiritual in very different ways – I find myself spending ninety per cent of my time in contented solitude, simply coming across others fortuitously, as it were. I can tread my own path, dissolve into the self, take stock, find union with the numinous and the earth.

What all this helps to do is focus attention on the natural world – both the retreat and the abbey possess surpassingly beautiful gardens, fields and orchards – and deepen my appreciation of the wild which lives within the tamed, the domestic, the cultivated.

When a new day dawns I want to be fully alive to it; I want to greet the rising sun; I want to find myself in the midst of songbirds and soft breezes; I want to bless the earth on which I stand and which helped make me, and makes me anew.

Every sunrise signifies rebirth, every day a lifetime encapsulated within a few meaningful and sometimes intense hours.

Within the manic activity, the ceaseless commotion, of the modern world, in which nerves are often stretched to breaking point and the blood boils; it is as well to take time out, get off the merry-go-round, and celebrate silence, stillness and solitude.

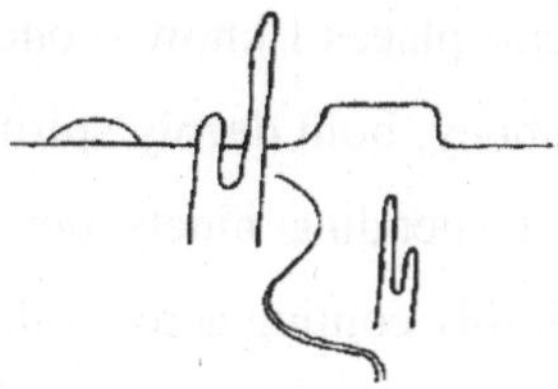

17 EDWARD ABBEY'S WILDERNESS

Within this landscape
cactus, mesa, snake, ravine:
the stilled desert's heart.

'The wild is as vital to our lives
as water and good bread.'

I like wilderness freaks hard-boiled – and they don't come more hard-boiled than Edward Abbey. I also like books which have a fine cutting edge at times, and at other times wield a primitive club. Edward Abbey's 'Desert Solitaire: A Season in the Wilderness' has both in wild and crazy abundance.

On the other hand, if you prefer your conservation, ecology, bioregionalism, nature communion and so on, larded with diplomacy and the niceties of good manners, then pass Desert

Solitaire by. But you will be missing something. This treatise possesses a kind of dynamite in the soul, a constructive anarchy and anger in response to the unpardonable depredations perpetuated by modern industrial society.

Edward Abbey, let it be said at the outset, doesn't mince words, nor does he suffer fools gladly. He is, or was, a very volatile man who witnessed the motor-home invasion of his beloved desert landscapes with horror and disgust. He saw the worst excesses of greed adopted as a way of life; it very nearly made him spew up his ice-cold Coors and put a foot through every television screen he could lay boots on. Certainly it got him into deep trouble with all those armchair conservationists who advocated a moderate, nuanced, compromise approach whilst the world continued to collapse about our ears. As he would say: This is no time for moderation!

In Desert Solitaire, Abbey fights for his own adopted patch – the south-western desert area of the USA. But really his remit is the earth, 'the only home we will ever have', as he poignantly put it.

In this book beauty sits uneasily alongside insanity: the beauty of land, sky, a transcendent human-animal-plant-rock relationship; the insanity of obtuse governments, rapacious corporations, polluting industry, camera-mad tourism and mindless human predation.

Abbey was a primitive, containing all the very best that that word implies. He was not a sophisticate, a crowd-pleaser or a 'progressive' in the sense of one who believes that humankind is making some sort of progress when, palpably, there is none. In Desert Solitaire he lays out the cards of his belief system, if pure, naked, unadulterated love of sand, sliprock and sunshine can ever constitute a belief system.

Much of the time he clearly prefers solitude to society, creekbeds to cities, and the primordial sounds of desert creatures to the trivial babble of human voices. Who can blame him? Switch on the television, radio, internet – what do you see and hear? Life at second- and third-hand. Who needs it?

Abbey tells us, by means of the quirky essay and personal history, that there is a world out there, a real world; a harsh, beautiful, delicate, robust, balanced, ecologically important and vital world which Homo Mechanicus has been turning his back on since the Industrial Revolution. It is a sorry sight. And yet, ironically, Abbey doesn't want too many people tramping over the remaining areas of wilderness. Easy access – air-conditioned coachloads at the Grand Canyon – means further degradation and misunderstanding of the natural world we have been blessed with. Somewhere along the line we bit the apple and it all began to go wrong. How in the hell do we get back to a state of grace?

Edward Abbey spent three seasons as a park ranger in south-eastern Utah. As he says in his introduction, 'What I found there is the subject of this book.' And he found a great deal that would undoubtedly be missed, or simply rejected, by the modern blinkered adult whose life is lived primarily in a series of enclosed artificial spaces, soothed by every manner of machine mediation. He found the great outdoors, nature in the raw, the poetry and pain of existence, something much greater than himself, much greater than all of us.

Abbey Speaks of Desert Solitaire being 'not primarily a book about the desert', although the message strikes us forcibly with the physicality of a sandstorm that the arid regions of the American south-west are the landscapes of his choice.

In the context of modern Western life, the desert – any desert – has a lot going for it: few people, a surprising complexity of flora and fauna, peace, quict, spacc for contemplation, relatively little eco-destruction, closeness to the Other (whatever that Other is conceived to be) – and not a single fast-food outlet, shopping mall or theme park. What more could a misanthrope want? And Abbey has been called that too, which is a profound misjudgement, because he loved people dearly, albeit in ones and twos rather than in football crowds.

Desert Solitaire is divided into a series of connected essays, some polemical, some anecdotal, some gently poetic, some fiercely controversial. But Abbey's writing is never dull. He may lull you into cosy agreement or outrage you with a mischievous suggestion. He is an extremist, an anarchist; subversive, heretic and naysayer, ornery challenger of the status quo; maddeningly self-contradictory at times, infuriatingly stubborn at other times; and then again charming in defence of wilderness. And, as we all know now, wilderness needs all the defenders it can get.

His prose style is muscular, racy, provocative, vernacular, intensely poetic and refreshingly unacademic. In his essay 'Down the River' he speaks of wilderness as being 'not a luxury but a necessity of the human spirit, and as vital to our lives as water and good bread. A civilization which destroys what little remains of the wild, the spare, the original, is cutting itself off from its origins and betraying the principle of civilization itself.'

Amen to that!

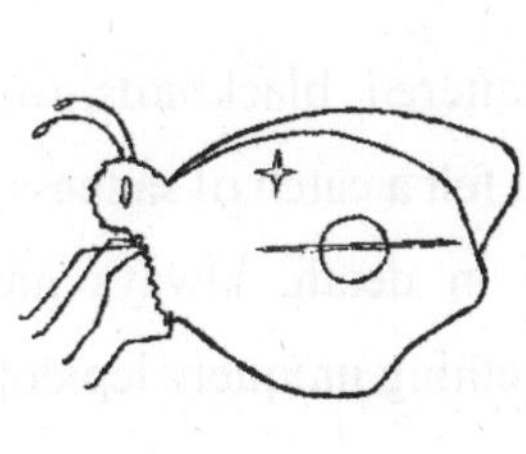

18 MAGICAL BUTTERFLY REVISITED

How admirable:
he who thinks not 'Life is short'
brings resurrection.

The deep orange bars and smudges have not appreciably faded. The little white oblongs near the wing tips are as white as ever. The ebony velvet of the body and the black dots embroidering the orange bars remain distinctive. Only the antennae have gone, the creature's once crucial sensors.

My imperfect watercolour of the Red Admiral retains its clarity but, I always think, represents a pale imitation of the real thing; the creature that one day fluttered down onto my lawn and never took off again. Six summers ago.

I recall the day now with absolute clarity: the wonder I felt, the frisson that ran through me. I have come across dead pigeons, feathers obscenely scattered, blackbirds, robins, even once a rat, on that same lawn and felt a catch of sadness for each. But the Red Admiral, spectacular in death, always meant something else, something more, something uniquely lepidopterous.

I think that this may relate to the paradoxical qualities of delicacy and strength, brevity and timelessness, freedom and confinement, motion and stillness. For butterflies freedom is confined within a few short hours; their brilliance dies almost as soon as they are born, like a miniscule flash of lightning or a slip of fleeting rainbow.

My desire is to see the Red Admiral as a stunning creation, even in death and embalmment; but butterflies, as with many creatures, suggest a potent symbolism.

I stare at my Red Admiral – *my* Red Admiral, I say, which is arguable in itself – and cannot help but cogitate on all the associations that butterflies suggest to us. Their capriciousness, their brilliance, their ephemerality, their fragility, their mesmerising dance, their brief settling and their seemingly random flitting away.

Some varieties grace the garden like tiny fragments of light energised and prismatic; some, single coloured, are sprites or spirits parking themselves on blooms and then rising, to be swept away on the breeze; some exotic varieties are almost surreal in contours and patterning.

An elderly lady, a local in this town, noticing that I was wearing a butterfly badge on my lapel, reacted with vociferous delight, which was somewhat disarming. I felt that I had been netted. 'Oh, you love butterflies too!' she exclaimed. 'Yes, I observe them, paint them and try, in my ignorance, to identify the different varieties. I am deeply fascinated by them.'

'Well,' she said, 'I have a collection of exotic butterflies and moths from South America, where my husband and I lived for some years. Would you like to give them a good home? We have no further use for them. They are properly mounted in a big glass display case. I'm sure you would appreciate them.'

I could not turn down such an offer, despite having serious reservations about butterfly collections: lepidopterists must net and kill these wondrous creatures and stick mounting pins through them, which seems brutal and almost blasphemous.

But, excited and weakening, I accepted her offer: the creatures were already dead. I am simply glad that my Red Admiral died naturally and no pins have ever been near it. It is lovingly preserved on a piece of tissue in a Perspex box (which I hesitate to call a sarcophagus) and greets me mutely every time I sit at my desk in the study, having pride of place.

On the subject of my butterfly badge, which over the years has attracted much attention from a variety of admirers: it was a gift from my wife and depicted a Peacock, whose two big wing spots always reminded me of an owl's eyes. Over time the colours printed on the badge faded. Don't we all fade in one way or another?

I used watercolours to revivify the tones and textures – and now the badge, worn proudly, elicits many intrigued comments once again. I conflate the butterfly badge with the Red Admiral at times, sensing the proximity of both.

Whenever I catch sight of a live Red Admiral, I am instantly reminded of the visionary creature I lifted off the lawn those six summers ago, and what it means to me now. I like to think that its spirit – however that may be interpreted – never died; that it lives on in all Red Admirals; that in preserving its form, colour, texture and essence, I have also preserved its meaning.

For in death there is not merely a finality – I don't think so – there is, rather, a change of state, a kind of occult resurrection. Although all things change, nothing is truly lost. That is the great and abiding paradox. The Earth, in common with people, preserves memories: tribal, folk, species' imprints.

When we are grounded, wounded, afflicted, made low and lame, we all wish to fly again. Disablement and death are no barrier, simply an entry into another world, a golden opportunity, a place beyond, that our limited minds cannot imagine but can strangely, liminally sense. There is a reality beyond and above that which we are capable of perceiving, and which in epiphanic moments we can touch.

I gaze long, newly fascinated, at the orange, white and black wings, the serrated contours, the velvety body, the stillness, the undemonstrative perfection of my Red Admiral. And it makes me feel as though, whenever I am heavily weighed down, I might fly again.

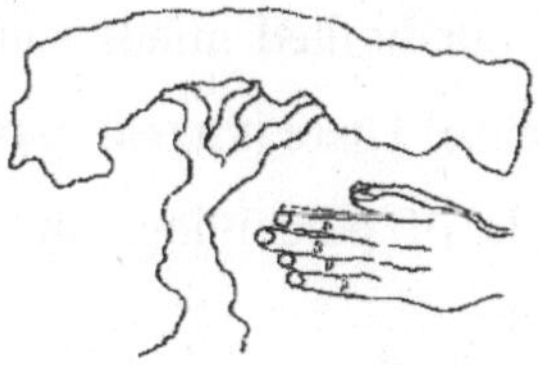

19 APPEASING THE TREE SPIRIT

Fallen fruit transforms
death to living energy
food for Eden's field.

I felt a great affinity with that tree; I still do. It stood until recently a mere thirty feet from the back of the house and loomed over the conservatory. It dominated the entire garden. The cedar was sixty feet high with a spread of perhaps forty feet. Its lowest boughs came within eight feet of the lawn on one side and dipped into a neighbour's garden on the other. It overcanopied not one but two sheds. It was hung with huge cones because it was November. It would never see another November. I was told –afterwards – that it had been about sixty years old. A tree surgeon counted the rings, a ring for every year of leaf fall and cone-bearing. The life history of the tree was at last exposed. The tree surgeon pointed out a two-inch length of metal buried deep inside the trunk, near the centre. Possibly the remains of a nail from an early nesting-box, he speculated.

For twelve years we have lived in the house, and for twelve years I have loved that cedar, despite the undoubted problems it caused. Its disadvantages were many: it shed so many needles that they smothered flower borders and paddled into the house; nothing much would grow under its huge canopy because it cut out light and absorbed so much groundwater; it obscured sunlight in summer, especially after midday and into early evening; and its low-hanging boughs dipped almost to head height. It was also getting bigger. The lovely cedar should have lived out a long, undisturbed life in a forest with many companions, many similar-sized giants, not hedged into a town garden.

For years I resisted the sound advice to have the tree felled; it made sense but also struck me – an inveterate tree-lover – as sacrilege, the wanton destruction of a magnificent living thing. My wife, as always, was more practical and less mystical about the issue of the cedar tree, although she appreciated it too. So a decision was made. The inevitable decision. The cedar tree was in the wrong place, despite the joy it engendered in me every day; despite its undoubted right to flourish and play host to collared doves and blue tits.

I had placed a nesting-box on its trunk about twenty feet from the ground. I recall blue tits using it as their home through several summers; I observed them day after day with a great uplift of the heart. Their antics were a sheer delight. But, of course, the nesting-box was the first thing to be removed and put away. That was the start of a startling transformation.

On many a late evening after dark, or an early morning before dawn, I would step into the garden and observe the embroidery of stars and, occasionally, catch sight of a full moon peeping through the branches of the cedar. It was a magical sight: the black filigree of the tree contrasting with the brilliance of the moon. It inspired me to produce a number of watercolours: tree and moon and the night sky. Zen moon. Snow moon. Harvest moon. At least I have the paintings now to remind me of what once existed there and how I felt about it. The full moon touched the cedar and touched me.

The tree surgeons were coming. This would be not so much an amputation as a dismemberment, a dissolution. I was compelled to accept the fact that all things change in the endless process of samsara, the cedar no different to animal existence; the blossoming and the fading and, in some esoteric way, rebirth.

I found some cones which had fallen onto the lawn only days before the tree surgeons' fateful visit. I had never come across such cones before; they were huge, heavy, sticky with resin, and one or two had tiny fragments of branch attached and needle-like splays of leaves.

I gathered them and took them to the greenhouse for safekeeping. The idea occurred to me that I might be able to germinate some of the offspring of the great cedar. If so, I would be careful not to plant them anywhere near the house, but perhaps cultivate them as bonsai; a poignant reminder of their parent tree who gave, by turns, so much joy and not a little consternation.

The tree surgeons arrived and wasted no time. We watched their amazing expertise in dismantling the cedar branch by branch, then leaving a bare trunk thirty feet high which reminded us of a totem pole. And that tree was certainly totemic, a natural symbol of something ultimately mysterious, worthy of restrained worship but destined to go the way of all material things. (I visualised the druids I had once seen in their long white robes placing soft hands against the huge trunk of an ancient yew and closing their eyes in a kind of quiet ecstasy, no doubt communing.) And 'tree huggers', environmental activists, who climbed high into magnificent mature trees in order to perch and challenge the axe-wielders to remove them before removing the trees. Such images flashed through my mind.

Was I condoning an act of sabotage, or perhaps a pointless

sacrifice? I don't think so. My heart told me to leave the cedar alone; my head told me that it would grow taller and wider by the year and eventually swamp our garden and maybe after that the neighbour's. Sometimes what seems brutal is unavoidable.

The tree surgeons, one scampering like a monkey or a circus acrobat all over the tree, made surprisingly short work of it. After they had sectioned the stout branches and the massive trunk – we baulked at the relentless whining of chainsaws – the resulting silence was absolute, and the entire garden was bathed in a heady fragrance of pine.

The ringed sections of cedar glistened with concentric circles of yellow and cream-coloured timber which had been invisibly embalmed inside the tree for decades; its life story told in one epidermis after another. It convinced me that even in death beauty is revealed.

Perhaps I was merely being fanciful, or fey. But surely there is more to material objects, whether animate or inanimate, than the surfaces which are presented to us? Surely there is a hidden life, the occult, realms remote from our own and generally inaccessible to us? In felling, in death, that cedar – *our* cedar – seemed to reveal its inner self, yielded its essence.

Before the tree surgeons left, the younger of the two made a curious comment. He said, 'I couldn't work in forests as a lumberjack; I love trees. It's just that this one was planted in the wrong place.' The irony of that comment struck me forcibly: a tree-feller who loves trees. Sometimes life is more complex that one imagines; it's too easy to misjudge people. What they do is not always what they believe. And, besides, what are we to do about things that are 'planted in the wrong place'?

When the garden had grown almost silent again after all the frenetic commotion and only birdsong threaded it with sound, I took a slow, mindful stroll about the lawn's perimeter. I reached the end of the garden, turned and looked back and was somewhat shocked not to see that great, dark, arboreal shape sweeping across the rooftops. Instead there was a cedar-shaped hole in the sky, a phantom of what had been. My sense of sight was temporarily befuddled and my sense of smell responded to the piquant resin of the quartered timbers, beguiled and astonished.

I held a surprisingly heavy cone in each hand and closed my eyes and imagined the great cedar tree as it once was. In my weakness I uttered a silent prayer of atonement.

I like to think that the tree spirit lives on in these few gathered cones, these embryos. Maybe, transformed, the cedar will live again.

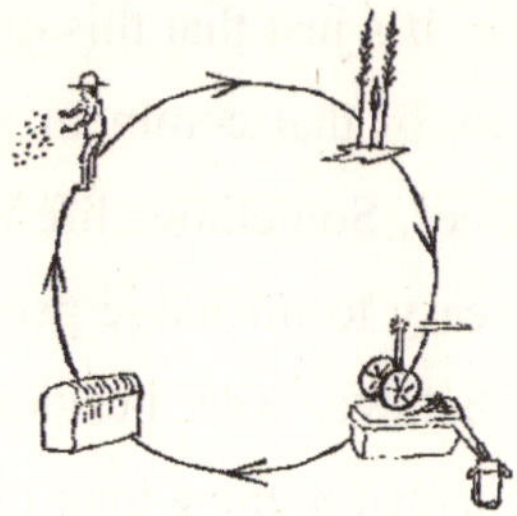

20 THE BREAD MATRIX

Behind this day's veil
lies interconnectedness:
you, me, everything.

I bake my own bread. Usually I am alone in the kitchen, but in reality such activity is a huge, collective effort. My mundane labours: mixing, kneading, proving, baking, displaying proudly on a wire cooling rack, are only the tail-end of a long and complex process. I have a great number of people to be grateful to; what is sometimes called the supply chain. Sometimes I think about them if I can persuade myself into a sufficiently meditative state of mind. Making my few loaves will not feed the five thousand, but behind this seemingly solitary process there may be many more than five thousand unwitting contributors.

Think about the number of people, most unseen, many unacknowledged, who in their own way and with consummate expertise contribute to every end product we can think of. It is too easy to say, 'I made this all on my own,' which is the kind of thing that, typically, children say with justified pride. And there is a touching validity in that. But what does 'all on my own' really mean? It cannot, surely, be literally true?

I contemplate my own bread-making. What, holistically, globally, is really involved? And how many people have made my deceptively simple act of baking possible?

A company produces wheat seed; a farmer procures the seed; a farmworker sows the seed; another farmworker, much later in the year, reaps the mature wheat; others gather the harvest and transport it.

These days, of course, with mechanised farming, workers with very different talents had to build the combine-harvesters and get them to the farms. Not to mention loaders and other essential pieces of equipment. And then imagine all the workers in the flour mills, grinding the wheat and packaging it.

I stand in my kitchen and, gingerly, peer into the oven to check that my bread dough is slowly, beautifully rising (sometimes I utter a prayer). Ah, yes, I had almost forgotten the yeast! How easy it is to forget something essential. A company's workers produced the yeast without which my bread would be decidedly unleaven – and disappointing!

I ought to mention dairy farmers, whose cows produced the milk which I include in my recipe; not to mention the Italian olive growers and transporters who produced the oil which I also add to the basic mixture of flour, water and yeast. I had almost forgotten the water! Water company workers toil to provide me and millions of others with fresh, clean water, which is essential to my bread and which, incidentally, we tend to take for granted. The potent combination of flour and water, such an unpromising looking 'mud', delights me every time.

Without sugar the yeast would have nothing to feed on, so cane or beet growers, and the processing companies, must receive due thanks. All are unsung heroes, even if I do not praise them except in moments like this.

When the loaves have proved and doubled in size, I switch on the oven, which itself is a product of multi-faceted manufacture. How many people did it take to provide the metal, glass, rubber and wiring which, artfully employed, went into the making of the oven in which my loaves begin to brown and crust? And at an earlier stage, before the work of those manufacturers, the scientists and designers? Perhaps I will never run out of people to thank!

I take a peek through the glass window of the oven door at my simple wholemeal loaves, which are not as 'simple' as I thought. The oven, of course, feels hot due to the electricity which powers it. More thanks are needed. I suppose I could go all the way back to Michael Faraday! Where on earth will my gratitude end?

In fact, if one adds to the long list of practical skills and expertise – from farmers to transporters to supermarkets – the somewhat less practical but equally essential skills of marketing, logistics, administration and finance; then the entire matrix of disciplines involved in the back-up to my home-baked bread becomes truly global, historical and almost overwhelming.

It is as if, in my own unobtrusive, almost invisible way, I am in human terms the end-product of a massive development, over time, of mind-boggling complexity.

I remove my apron. I sit gazing at the risen loaves cooling on the wire rack. I cannot help feeling a little self-satisfied. And yet my part in the creation of wholesome wholemeal bread has been but one small labour, one finite skill, in a vast matrix of human effort.

I wish each one of those people could bite into a slice of my warm bread topped with butter – but I'm afraid I haven't sufficient loaves to feed the five thousand!

21 A FEW YELLOW FLOWERS

Outgoing swallow,
what instinct fires migration,
what end draws your flight?

I'd had the bonsai forsythia for at least three years. It had never produced flowers, although each year it boasted plenty of rich green foliage. I knew that it flowered in winter, which I regarded as a rare bonus, considering the relative paucity of bright blossoms in that season of general dormancy. But in nature there is always magic if one actively seeks it. And patience brings its own reward.

It was mid-December when I brought the bonsai forsythia into the house from my small end-of-garden greenhouse. I wanted to encourage it, perhaps induce a spurt of growth, even though I was well aware that this plant happily flowers in the depths of winter, despite its delicate appearance. We all know how deceptive appearances can be. I recalled seeing well-established forsythia bushes against walls and fences, bedecked with exquisite yellow flowers and dusted with snow.

So, placing the tiny oblong trough on a relatively warm kitchen window sill may have seemed counter-intuitive. But I felt protective, and in any case I couldn't keep an eye on the little thing if it were stuck in a remote greenhouse along with a host of much larger, overwintering potted plants. (I keep many other bonsai in that greenhouse, that I know would have no hope of flowering until the following summer, which is as it should be: each thing in its season.)

The forsythia was no more than four inches tall and as many wide. I had pruned it meticulously into a loose kind of box shape. Its stems were spiky, truncated by my pruning. There were tiny buds, barely visible, along each of the stems, which encouraged me to believe that, one day soon, it might just flower. But I did not hold my breath. This almost bare, insignificant-looking plant would flourish only when it was ready to do so, despite my earnest ministrations. That is one of the many wonderful things about nature: it will go on at its own pace, often resisting the encouragement and, indeed, interference of humans.

We can produce hybrids, manipulate shape, size, perfume, develop gigantic specimens for shows and so on; but with all of these things we must also cultivate patience. We must slow ourselves down to the pace which, to many who insist on instant gratification, is no doubt frustrating. Gardeners, but more particularly bonsai experts, of which I am not one, understand the rhythms of plants within the encompassing rhythms of the seasons.

Anyway, the dark days of December progressed and approached Christmas. I glanced at the kitchen window sill several times a day, noting any minor changes in the forsythia. There were none – not at first. Its little spiky stems, which I had earlier taken the secateurs to, looked bare, almost pathetic. I began to feel guilty at performing even minor surgery on this delicate live thing which could not speak for itself, not protest. (It might be truer to say that it spoke in other than human terms.) I felt that perhaps I had failed with this particular bonsai; that I should have left it in the greenhouse to take its chance with all the others. Why should I intervene? What was I doing?

At the end of the third week of December I noticed that the insignificant buds, only three out of perhaps four times that many, had swelled noticeably. I became encouraged, even a tiny bit excited, which is unlike me. I sprinkled a few drops of water onto the shallow bed of compost in the trough, which had developed a beautiful mossy carpet on its surface. The main stem of the forsythia poked through this green patina at a slight angle before bifurcating once and then again and again to form a miniature crown – but not a crown of thorns!

Christmas Day arrived and I had plenty to do. In my busyness I had almost forgotten the bonsai forsythia which sat neglected on the kitchen window sill. But then, in the midst of considerable culinary commotion, I caught sight of something: a single, tiny yellow flower breaking into bloom. On Christmas morning! I could hardly believe the timing! On this of all days. It felt like one birth complementing another. It felt as if that bonsai 'knew' when would be the most propitious moment to flower, although I am well aware that this is a somewhat fanciful idea.

In the days following Christmas Day two more miniscule flowers appeared, perfect examples of winter-flowering forsythia. There are many things to be grateful for: cards and presents, good food and the birth of a child; family and friends and carols and ceremonies. But it strikes me that the little things, the things that people often overlook, add beauty and significance to the world.

My bonsai forsythia is flowering still, if not on its stems, then in my spirit.

22 MEDITATING ON A SNAIL

The fragrance of life
lingers in this little jot:
love invisible.

It is early January, the weather bitterly cold. In such low temperatures it takes a brave soul to spend much time in the garden. Like many other people at this time of year, post-festive season, I semi-hibernate, at least in the hours of darkness. It is the way of many animal species, and it must have been the way of our ancestors: hunker down around the fire, sleep and dream of balmier, lighter, more active days.

In modern times we seem to have lost that ancient circadian rhythm due to modern work patterns, artificial light, instant entertainment and so on. But the very idea of winter hibernation, of slowing down, reassessing life, regenerating one's vital energies, appeals to me enormously. It seems healthy, common sense, an antidote to the all too often manic pace of modern life.

As Ark Redwood says in his inspiring book, The Art of Mindful Gardening, 'I actually love the winter. I cherish it for its simplicity as animals and plants withdraw into themselves.' I sympathise with Ark in that sentiment. But there are a few things one needs to do in the wintry, all but closed down garden, even under a blanket of snow.

This morning at first light, crunching over a frosty surface, I walk to the big greenhouse. I am protected against the bitter chill, as I know many potted plants are similarly protected in the confines of the greenhouse. I do my best to nurture them at each time of year, according to the season's unique conditions.

Inside the greenhouse I can hardly move, so full is it of potted trees and shrubs which at other times of year would glory in space, freedom, the open and unglazed benediction of the sun.

I have come to check on a few things, reaching the door of the plants' seasonal resting place, their temporary dormitory, their refuge of hidden, subdued but nonetheless continuing life. It occurs to me that so much potential for further growth, for a sublime quickening of life, for the miraculous resurgence of leaf and blossom, is harboured within those dead-looking trunks and stems and branches. Therein lies a metaphor for hope in perhaps the most straitened of circumstances, for a blossoming of the spirit against all the odds.

Once inside the greenhouse I study each plant in turn, noting its bareness and, in some cases, its tenacious and heartening fecundity. Even in the depths of winter the vestiges of last summer's spectacular display of foliage remains, although the petals from late blossoming – the dry, crinkly purple of bougainvillea, for example – lie scattered about the central path. I wonder whether to give a drink of water to compost which is clearly desert-dry; but then I think, no, those plants are dormant, quiescent, patiently awaiting the thaw and the first stirrings of spring. They don't need a kickstart yet.

One sinuous, straggly plant has almost outgrown its pot, as capacious as the pot is. Perhaps next year I will treat it to the freedom of an open border, a high fence against which to display its tiny, beguilingly fragranced flowers. Summer jasmine in its pared-down winter coat, which makes it looks oddly scarecrow-like, ragged but eccentrically charming.

I touch the tendrils and the curling leaves, which wind about each other in a kind of verdant matrix, as though the climber clings to itself for dear life; as though it would do what hibernating mammals do and adopt the same foetal position which preceded their birth.

The analogy strikes me as intriguing: curled up in dormancy, a poignant reflection of that pre-natal curvature, like clockwork ready to mark time in the ticking around the heavens of sun and moon. Of course this summer jasmine developed from a seed or a cutting; its gestation occurred in the womb of a tiny pot. But, germinated, it would have sprung forth from the seed and curled upwards, blind at first but seeking light and warmth; searching for life as we search for some kind of spiritual sustenance.

I examine the summer jasmine further and, half hidden inside a curled leaf, catch sight of a tiny snail clinging on. It captures my attention, that anonymous jot of life, everything else in the world unaware of it. How long has it been here?

I stare at the snail, trying to comprehend something beyond myself, something which eludes rational thought, some intimate but paradoxically holistic connection. Oddly, I feel an ineffable emotion when I see that miniscule creature just clinging to a leaf, riding out the winter, disinclined to move, to risk itself. I feel protective, almost tender. There's something about these plants resting in the greenhouse, this snail and myself, a synergy which goes way beyond a chance encounter.

I think my unexpected emotion, which I confess others might mock or be amused by, points to a truth which we ignore at our peril: an abiding sensitivity which ensures that we do no harm. That surely is the mantra: do no harm. It is, if you like, not a matter of logic or intellect, or even ethics – but a matter of soul.

Lately I have felt again and again that, rather than perceiving ourselves and all sentient and, for that matter, all insentient beings as separate, isolated, alone in an incomprehensible universe; we are one flux, one energy, one being, one mind, miniscule fragments of the whole, utterly dependent on each other. That is a warming, indeed inspiring, thought – in winter as much as any other time.

The universe can be seen and felt as one undivided and unbroken whole. Surely moments of epiphany, in this case sparked by a snail, convince us of the truth of this. Surely in meditation, when we sink deeply into the core of our being, that transcendent sense of Oneness becomes gloriously apparent. That, I think, is why meditation is so refreshing: it opens our eyes to things we have become temporarily blinded to. But here I digress.

The snail sits suspended before me, inside the tangled and contorted body of the summer jasmine, sustained and supported by it. I study it a little closer. Its shell comprises whorls of beige and ivory; there is none of the customary slate grey. It is a thing of beauty, a living jewel; so tiny, so seemingly insignificant, so closed within itself – and yet, I realise, it forms a part of me and you and the one mind of the universe. I feel honoured and humbled as I leave the greenhouse. I gaze up at a brightening blue sky and something beyond thought changes in me.

When I meditate I shall focus my concentration on that snail and pray that I might find myself once again, the soft inner core beneath the hard shell.

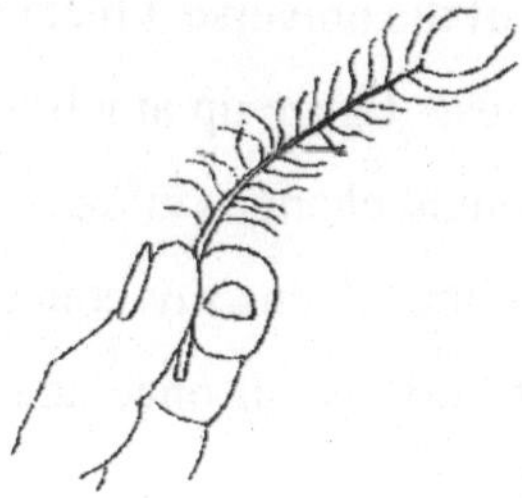

23 FLIGHT TO FREEDOM

Earlier than speech,
touch tells of love's unity,
life's first word and last.

I had left the door of the shed wide open. When I entered I heard a tiny commotion high up in one corner where two windows join at right angles. A moment of panic. Something was up there, something that I had inadvertently cornered. I caught little flashes of bright colour: blue and yellow, a glaze of sudden movement, a vigorous fluttering back and forth across a window pane. Perhaps a bid for freedom.

Don't we all at times have that? The sense of being trapped? A sudden craving for release beyond the glass, the four walls, the straitjacket of routine? The sight of something alluring which we cannot, despite a desperate struggle, reach?

I advanced to a far corner of the shed where tiny wisps of feather seemed suspended in air – and there it was, a confusion of canary yellow, ultramarine, white and black. A blue tit, scrabbling like mad from one window to the next, its manic whirr of wings giving the blue and yellow an illusion of green, like an artist's swirl of colours.

I held my hand up slowly in contrast to the dashing and diving of the tiny bird. I cupped my hands and, when the bird had settled momentarily, throbbing, clinging, brought them together like soft, solicitous pincers. The bird seemed at that moment to give up its struggle to reach the familiar landscape of the garden, the wide open spaces; seemed to submit to an uncertain fate.

I brought my cupped hands together as gently as I could, enclosing the exquisite fluffball of blue, yellow and white-black contrasts; it panicked once more as it found itself entombed. It was a baby blue tit, more naïve, perhaps, than its parents; a lost wanderer drawn to the shed.

Something inside me roused up in a kind of protective emotion, a desire to connect in some unfathomable way to the life of this bird. I opened my hands gingerly, lifting a finger like a trapdoor opening in a ball of flesh. The bird's head lay motionless, its glamorous wings having given up the struggle, or so it seemed.

I felt a physical warmth, a heartbeat, the bird's pulse seeming to communicate through the flesh of my palms, reassuring at least to me if not to this disorientated and no doubt terrified creature.

I turned with the bird inside the claustrophobic ball of my hands – I imagined horses and hawks quietened by the simple application of a blindfold – and left the shed and stepped into the open reaches of the garden.

The baby blue tit seemed to have become quiescent. I thought back to the collared dove I had placed hands upon months before, a much bigger bird but equally soft and silky.

I opened my hands with infinite care, like a prised clam revealing a tiny ball of pulsing vivid colour. The blue tit seemed stunned, fazed by new light, the natural habitat denied to it for a brief time. I looked closely at the pinpoint black dot of the eye which was uppermost. It seemed inscrutable, no doubt aware of this monstrous alien face looming above it, this would-be predator.

Then, in the blink of an eye, it flew. My eyes followed the blue tit for a breath-held moment before it weaved over the hedge and was gone forever. What remained in my half-cupped hands were little filigrees of down, a single poignant pale blue tail feather, which I wish the bird had taken with it. No matter. It escaped the shed, a kind of transient captivity, and it escaped me.

I lifted the slither of tail feather meticulously between thumb and index finger and held it up to the sky. It was semi-transparent, shivered in the breeze and matched the swathe of blue sky above me.

That baby blue tit, insignificant as it seemed, taught me a valuable lesson: when all seems lost, when the world closes around you, when there comes a distinct prospect of final moments – remember that the lure of freedom always calls; that hope remains; that seeming frailty can transform into miraculous strength.

24 ONE FLOCK, ONE MIND

Days of settled dusk,
great armadas of songbirds
perform miracles.

I have long been in the habit of sky-gazing. Clouds, moon, sun, rainbows, even high-flying aircraft, fascinate me. It is difficult to determine quite why. So much space – and none of it really 'empty'. That is a myth: the 'emptiness of space'. Space is not so much a vacuum as a vast and boundless reservoir of energy. Standing in my garden and simply looking up connects me with all those elements of the sky. Whilst my eyes appreciate the heavens, my feet are grounded in solid earth.

I like to imagine the sky, the infinity of space, as consisting of a single, complex, mysterious and beautiful mind. A kind of divinity, if you will. But I wish to foreshorten the focus away from the starry heavens to a stratum much closer to earth; to be precise only fifty to a hundred feet above the rooftops of the houses which surround my garden. The domain of birds. But I am thinking of a specific species of bird.

During my dreamy episodes of sky-gazing I have observed many times lately a kind of aerial ballet put on during that time of day we humans call dusk, but birds perhaps sense as something else: the softening and deepening of light. It is curious that, unlike humans, they do not have the words but feel the sensations. That is another kind of language.

Untroubled by traffic, the solidity of architecture and numerous physical impediments at ground level, birds glory in the freedom of the untrammelled. There is little to stop them showing off, as it were, if they wish to put on a performance of some elaborate dance just a short distance above firmly anchored trees and rooftops.

I love to bear witness to the flights of all birds; many species are distinctive and unmistakeable in their habits of movement and gesture, from the dive-bombing of gulls to the helicopter-hovering of kestrels to the slow-motion wing-flapping of herons and the technicolor darting of finches. But I am thinking of much more 'ordinary' birds; birds which would hardly win beauty contests or singing competitions. Namely, starlings. Unsung heroes, en masse, of the near firmament.

For some time this year I have made a crepuscular study of these flocks, or murmurations, as they gather and perform their amazing, synchronised aerial acrobatics above my house and garden and the nearby woods, avoiding any earthbound structures which appear beneath their dizzying orbit.

It is astonishing, almost breathtaking, to bear witness to the antics of huge gatherings of starlings as they career about the heavens, at one moment above my head, at the next almost vanishing above woodland a quarter mile away and then returning at breakneck speed. I could not possibly count them, even if I wanted to, so swift and interlacing are their movements, with such glorious and dynamic perpetual motion; but I would guess that perhaps a hundred starlings perform together just as the light of day is beginning to fade.

They do not remain in one large flock but split into two as if at some esoteric signal and then hurtle off in opposite directions. And soon, following a great wheel in the sky, one half of the flock splits again, so splinter groups are formed at dazzling speed, scattering in all directions, circling, blending, criss-crossing, now head on, now diving down and sweeping aloft.

But what strikes me as most remarkable of all as I observe these manic, freewheeling flocks, which reflect light as they turn and remind me of so many black splinters, whizzing, exploding, out of some chunk of slate or ebony; what really fascinates me is that they all move with one mind.

It is as if a hundred separate brains and bodies operate as one organism, instantly, to an invisible signal. No single starling falters or loses rhythm. It is, as I recall, precisely the same phenomenon with shoals of fish who, in their very different element, turn this way and that as one, performing a stupendous submarine ballet.

Observing the antics of these showoff starlings – which, incidentally, many pedestrians whose vision remains stubbornly horizontal seem blissfully unaware of – really reinforces in my own mind how deeply and mysteriously interlinked we all are; how understanding and communication go beyond language, beyond conscious choreography, into some gnomic realm; and how really being mindful of natural phenomena pays lasting dividends.

I thank those starlings both for their dynamic aerial display and for the unwitting lessons they teach.